# They call me *Lopez*

## *A Saga of Wilderness Flying*

William Lopaschuk

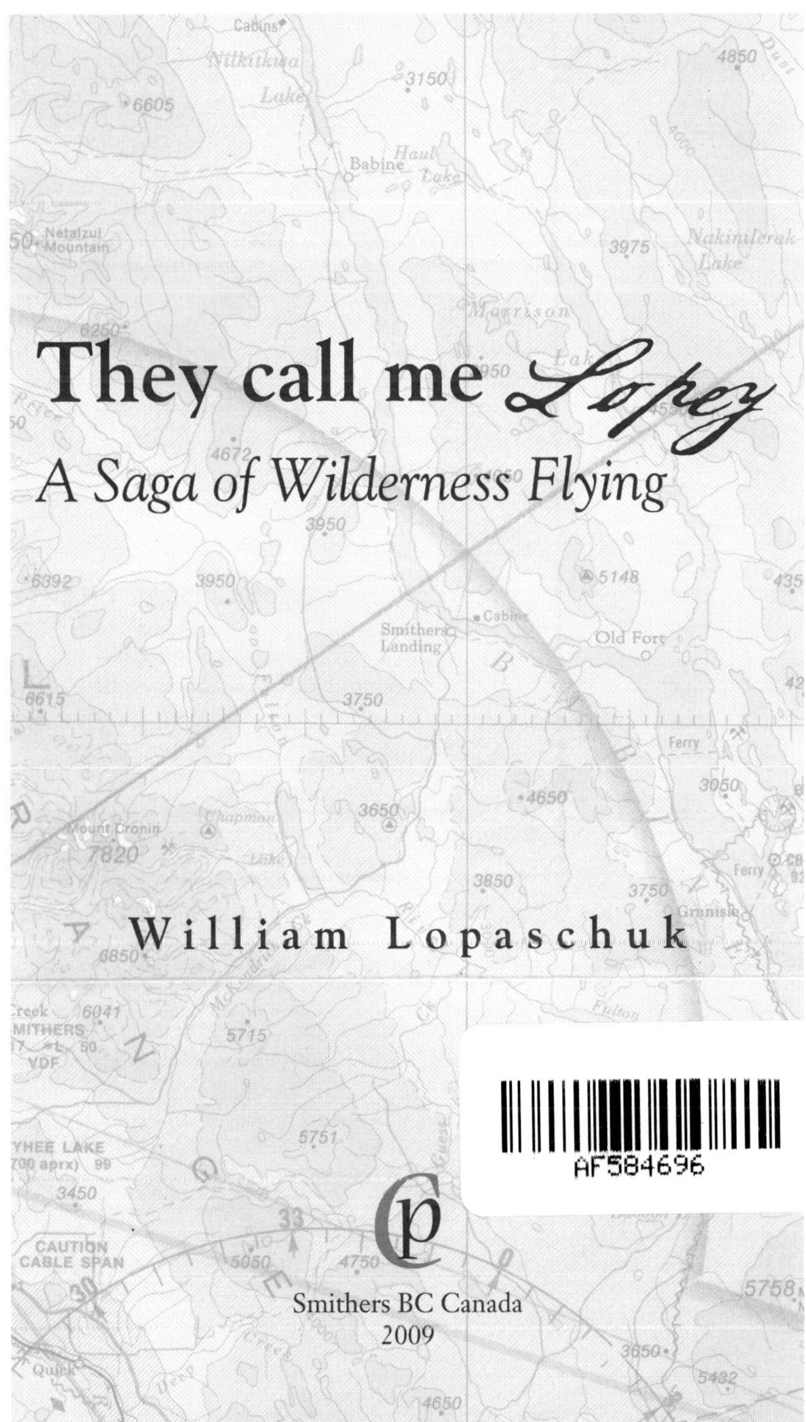




cp

Smithers BC Canada
2009

Creekstone Press, 7456 Driftwood Road
Smithers BC V0J 2N7 Canada
www.creekstonepress.com



Library and Archives Canada Cataloguing in Publication
Lopaschuk, William, 1927-
They call me Lopey : a saga of wilderness flying / William Lopaschuk.
ISBN 978-0-9783195-2-6
1. Lopaschuk, William, 1927-. 2. Bush pilots--British Columbia--Biography. 3. British Columbia--Biography. I. Title.
TL540.L66A3 2009 629.13092 C2009-903604-5

Editor: Lynn Shervill
Design: ArcheType Enterprises
Cover Design: Hans Saefkow
Maps: Andree MacKay

Most of the photos, unless otherwise credited, were taken by Bill Lopaschuk or by friends with his camera. If further information is available please contact info@creekstonepress.com.

The cover photo shows, from left to right, Roy McDougall, storekeeper at Finlay Forks, trapper Ed Stranberg, and the author. They are standing on the frozen Finlay River near the forks, now under the waters of the Williston Reservoir.

They Call Me Lopey is typeset in Janson Text and printed and bound by Friesens in Canada on paper made from trees harvested from sustainable forest practices and produced chlorine and acid free.

*For Toni*

*children Randy, Gary and Lynn*

*grandchildren Owen, Mark, David, Tim, Lauren and Erica*

*and for our angel,*

*Sarah*

# Contents

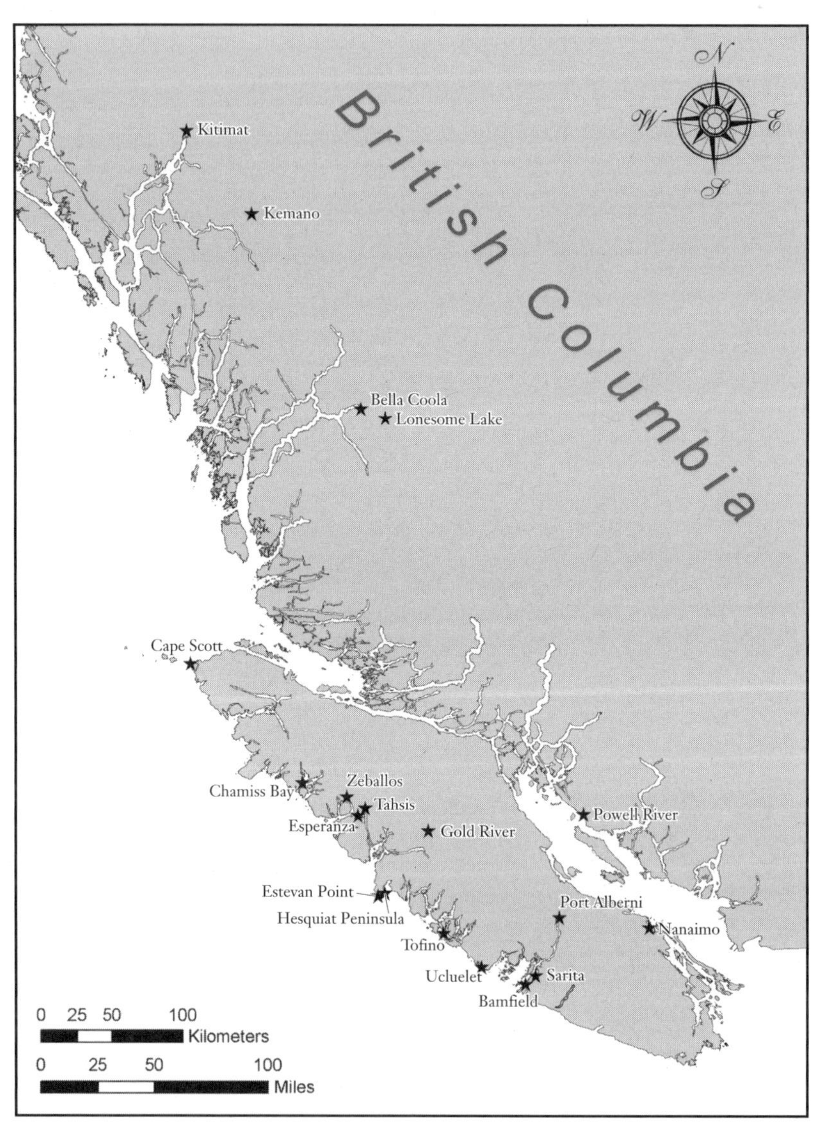
British Columbia
N
W
E
S
Kitimat
Kemano
Bella Coola
Lonesome Lake
Cape Scott
Chamiss Bay
Zeballos
Tahsis
Esperanza
Gold River
Powell River
Estevan Point
Hesquiat Peninsula
Tofino
Port Alberni
Nanaimo
Ucluelet
Sarita
Bamfield
0 25 50 100
Kilometers
0 25 50 100
Miles

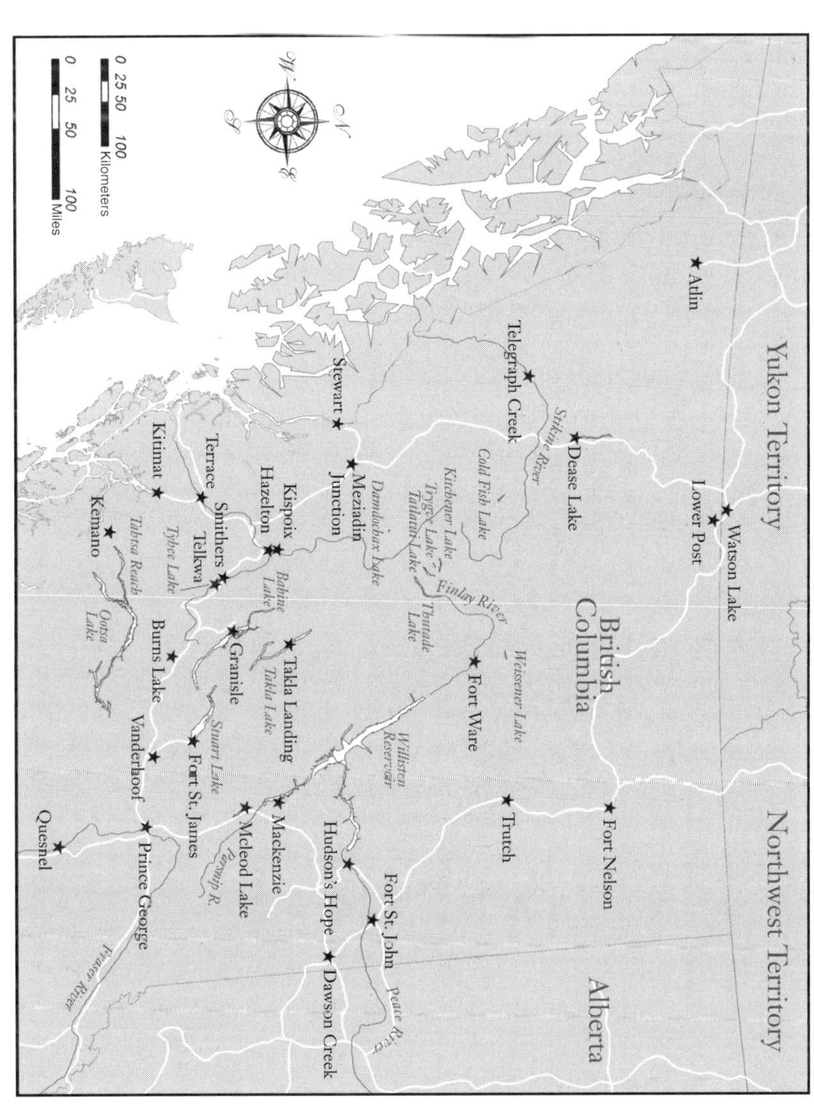
Yukon Territory
Northwest Territory
British Columbia
Alberta
Atlin
Watson Lake
Lower Post
Telegraph Creek
Dease Lake
Stikine River
Cold Fish Lake
Kitchener Lake
Trygve Lake
Tatlatui Lake
Finlay River
Thutade Lake
Weissener Lake
Fort Ware
Williston Reservoir
Fort Nelson
Trutch
Fort St. John
Hudson's Hope
Dawson Creek
Peace River
Stewart
Meziadin Junction
Damdochax Lake
Kispoix
Hazelton
Babine Lake
Takla Landing
Takla Lake
Granisle
Smithers
Telkwa
Terrace
Kitimat
Kemano
Tahtsa Reach
Tyhee Lake
Ootsa Lake
Burns Lake
Stuart Lake
Fort St. James
Vanderhoof
Mackenzie
Mcleod Lake
Parsnip R.
Prince George
Quesnel
Fraser River
0 25 50 100 Kilometers
0 25 50 100 Miles

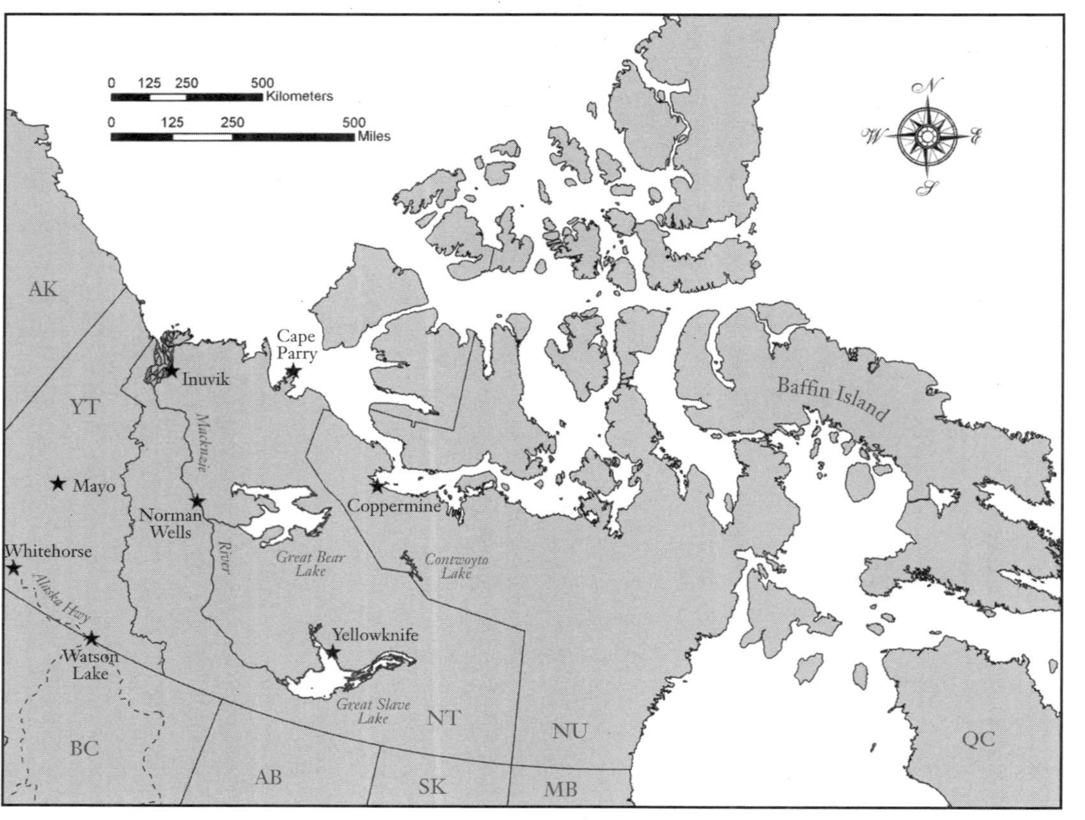
0 125 250 500
Kilometers
0 125 250 500
Miles
N
W
E
S
AK
YT
Inuvik
Cape Parry
Mackenzie
River
Mayo
Norman Wells
Whitehorse
Alaska Hwy
Watson Lake
BC
AB
SK
MB
NT
NU
QC
Great Bear Lake
Coppermine
Contwoyto Lake
Yellowknife
Great Slave Lake
Baffin Island

# Foreword

I have known Bill Lopaschuk for more than 40 years. But early on we conversed more over Aeradio than face to face. No longer. Over the years our professional relationship has evolved into a solid friendship. And now – both of us retired – we can sit and chat in close proximity.

During my 30-year career with Transport Canada I met an untold number of pilots from Sunday flyers to airline captains. And, while I enjoyed a good rapport with all of them, I identified closely with a special breed of aviators – bush pilots. They have been called barnstormers and daredevils, and they shared adjectives like hardworking, resourceful, independent and competent. Some were cautious, others happy-go-lucky. But all loved flying. And none more so than the unassuming man they call Lopey.

Bill flew on wheels or skis or floats over terrain devoid of navigational aids and mostly out of radio contact with ground stations. And while he willingly accepted challenges, he early on recognized that a pilot being old and bold was an oxymoron.

But there was another side to Bill's love affair with airplanes. He not only flew them; he also wanted to build them. And he did. Over seven winters, guided by a plan and an idea, using metal, wood, fibreglass and fabric, he built himself a small, two-seater. After he installed a four-cylinder, water-cooled engine all that was needed was a prop, probably the most intricate component of an aircraft. Unless the two halves are absolutely identical, the seven foot appendage will shake the aircraft to pieces. That's why props are bought. Only Lopey carved it himself from a laminated slab of birch.

Bill Lopaschuk has been called a genius. I prefer the term "Renaissance man."

Walter Hromatka
April 2009

# Introduction

In my years as a bush pilot I have logged over 17,000 hours of flying time and between 25,000 and 30,000 takeoffs and landings. Most were uneventful but some were not. For instance, I hit a 30-foot basking shark on takeoff from the Sarita River docks near Bamfield on the west coast of Vancouver Island, landed in a swamp north of Fort St. James with a seized engine, and tore the landing gear off a twin-engine Widgeon during an emergency landing near Fort St. John. I have flown air ambulance missions and mineral surveys, fought forest fires, and made supply runs for most of the major power developments in northern BC, including the Kemano project and the Williston Reservoir. I have flown planes from 18 manufacturers and at least 60 individual aircraft, including the first de Havilland Beaver (CF-FHB) to come off the assembly line. My first flying lesson was in 1947 in a Cessna 140 and I bought my first plane, a war-surplus Cornell trainer, in 1949 for $625. I have worked for a variety of airline companies, including Trans-Provincial, Central BC Airways, and Pacific Western and been based in communities stretching from Vancouver to the Dew Line on the Arctic shore. I last worked as a commercial pilot in 1978 but flew privately for another 30 years. What follows I wrote so that my family, especially my children and grandchildren, would have some record of my life. I hope you enjoy it too.

William Lopaschuk
2009

# A Trial to My Mother

My first experience with airplanes was in Whitehorse in 1935 when I was eight years old. We lived in a rented house near the airport and whenever I heard a plane I would climb up a trail towards the runway, day or night, so I could see it. I once saw seven Japanese bombers come in for refuelling. Horse-drawn wagons carrying big fuel drums pulled up beside the planes and gas was pumped into the tanks by hand.

I could tell my mother was uncomfortable with this obsession for airplanes but my father actually tried to arrange for me to go up with one of the Yukon bush pilots. It was not to be. Mother absolutely forbade any such foolishness on the grounds it was too dangerous. It would be many years before I climbed into my first plane but I always wondered what that bush pilot might have thought had he taken me up and then later found out I had followed in his footsteps.

I was born at home April 18, 1927 to George Lopaschuk and his wife Vera (nee Bilan) in Vernon, BC, the second of five children. My parents moved to the Okanagan Valley from central Saskatchewan and had their first child, Wilma, in 1925. Shortly after my arrival came Doreen. Richard and Marilyn, the latecomers, were born in 1943 and 1945 respectively.

Initially Dad worked for a rail company on the line between Vernon and Kelowna but when that job ended, during the early years of The Depression, he and his brother Bill moved to the Yukon and started fur trapping. Mom, my two sisters and I moved in with my paternal grandparents in Lone Butte, a little farming community near 100 Mile House in the Cariboo. I started school there and one of the first things I learned was about double jeopardy. I poked my ruler into the back of the boy in front of me and got the strap. Then, when I got home, my mother gave me a spanking for the same misdeed, my sister Wilma having ratted me out. It was a good lesson and had future implications as one mistake in an airplane could have many consequences, not to mention the mountains of paperwork that followed any accident.

*Bill's parents, George and Vera Lopaschuk, in the Okanagan Valley.*

Dad made enough money trapping during his first winter to keep himself and us in groceries. In the spring he landed a job with the White Pass & Yukon Railroad, working as a carpenter on the company docks and river boats along the Yukon River between Whitehorse and Dawson City. As an adjunct to this job, the railroad also hired him to deliver gold mined in the Dawson City area from the paddle wheelers to company trains in Whitehorse for shipment to the East. These jobs earned him enough money to bring his family north to Whitehorse.

I loved that trip. Taking the train from Lone Butte to Vancouver, sailing on the Grand Trunk Pacific luxury liner *Prince Rupert* to Skagway, riding the legendary White Pass & Yukon train to Whitehorse, eating in a restaurant and staying in a hotel – these were all thrilling firsts for

*Bill and his sister, Doreen, outside their home in Whitehorse.*

this wide-eyed boy from the Interior. I can still remember one of the menu items from the restaurant in Carcross, a stop on the rail line to Whitehorse. It was groundhog stew. Mother declined.

June days in Whitehorse never ended and I loved it. But not my mother. She could never get me to come in. I remember one night hearing her call out, "Billy (I hated being called Billy), time for bed." I was riding my scooter along the boardwalk and deliberately ignoring my mother. Instant karma – the front wheel of my scooter caught in a crack in the boardwalk. I fell and tore a hole in my new, 75-cent overalls and my knee. Now I had three problems. I hadn't listened to my mother, I'd torn my overalls (worth two hours work by my father) and, worst of all, when mother saw my knee she'd be really worried.

It was all too much for me. There was no way to fix my coveralls and the water for cleaning the gash in my knee was in the house. I went in, was severely scolded, and then loaded on a bicycle which my father wheeled to the hospital where I got about six stitches.

While Whitehorse was a good place for my dad to earn a living, it was also kind to me. If I met the trains and boats coming into town I could make about 25 cents a trip taking tourists to attractions like Sam McGee's cabin. I could also make money by collecting whiskey bottles. The local

*Bill, far right, and other Whitehorse major-leaguers on the sandlot.*

stores used them to supply residents of Whitehorse with kerosene for their lamps. The storeowners would buy the bottles from me, fill them from their 45-gallon drums and then sell them to the citizens. The town did have electricity but that was a luxury beyond the reach of most homeowners. Harassing newlyweds was another source of capital. Once we figured out where they were staying, the local kids would kick up such a racket the groom would usually give us some money to go away. In the summer of 1937 I earned just over $15, enough to pay for all my winter clothes, Christmas presents for my family and a model airplane kit from the Eaton's catalogue.

As a family, we spent three years in Whitehorse and then moved back to the Okanagan in 1938. Dad continued to work in the Yukon for a few summers, but spent the winters with us. We moved into a rental place in Enderby while Dad bought some land near Vernon, 16 acres on the Silver Star Road about a half mile north of the main highway, and started to build us a house. As it was the start of World War Two Dad was hired to build some armed forces barracks in Vernon and then to maintain them during the war years. He would work at his government carpentry job during the day, earning a whopping $1 an hour, and then work on our house in the evenings. On the weekends he rode a bicycle back to Enderby to spend time with his family.

As the adult labour force was greatly diminished during the war years, students spent only eight months a year in school instead of 10. The extra two months we were out in the orchards. I was able to get work as a teamster's helper in a nearby apple orchard, a job that paid 10 cents an hour more than the going rate of 25 cents an hour for a high school student. We thinned the trees in June and picked in September. I would arrive an hour early in the morning and stay an extra hour at night to care for the horses. And, of course, there was always a lot to do at home. We had cows, chickens and a good sized garden which tended to offset the privations of wartime rationing. In fact, we were even able to make a little money selling milk, butter and sugar fruits to the city dwellers. I can remember my sister Wilma and me walking to the local store, each with a dozen eggs in a paper bag. The store owner would give us a penny a piece for the eggs, enough for a movie and two cents for candy.

We also had a Model T Ford but with gas rationing there had to be a very good reason to put it on the road. So Dad did a makeover on the car. He cut out the back seat and built a wooden box to fit the empty space, thus converting the family car into a farm truck and qualifying for an extra fuel ration.

After the war ended I worked in a garage for a few years, acquiring the mechanical knowledge that later proved very beneficial to my flying career. The immediate benefit, however, was enough knowledge to build a tractor from an old vehicle chassis and spare parts destined for the junk pile. Now, instead of having to hire a horse team, we had a vehicle with which to harvest the hay crops. First we'd use the tractor to pull the mechanical mower. Then, once the hay was cut, we'd pile the hay onto a stone boat and pull it to the barn with the tractor.

Working with vehicles also enabled me to make a major contribution to the family tie-cutting business. My dad, Wilma's husband Bob, and I purchased an old portable sawmill that was powered by a six cylinder Buick engine. I looked after the engine overhaul and Bob and Dad rebuilt the mill to operational standards. The mill, however, was only good for squaring the railroad ties. The trees still had to be felled and limbed by hand. I became quite handy with cross cut and Swede saws and a double bitted axe.

We cut ties at various locations in the Vernon area during the week and would then return home for the weekend. One Friday, on our way home, I noticed a brand new aircraft sitting in a field. Nothing would do but to stop and have a look. It was a Fleet Canuck just out of the factory, a beautiful machine. I told my dad I would like to learn to fly. "Well," he said, "you always go on a holiday. Why don't you stay home and learn to fly instead." That was it. On August 3, 1947, just turned 20, I had my first flying lesson.

# Flying Solo and Double

I soon discovered that what I spent on a holiday didn't go far towards obtaining a pilot's licence. It took me a year to purchase enough lessons to make instructor Dan McIvor feel comfortable letting me fly solo. I will always remember that day – June 2, 1948. Dan just stepped out of the aircraft – a new Cessna 140 trainer – and informed me I was on my own. I spent the next thirty minutes doing circuits of the airfield at the Vernon airport. My total dual-instruction time was 12 hours.

My eventual goal was to obtain a commercial pilot's licence but this would require a total of 250 hours airtime. After logging 34 expensive hours in the rented Cessna trainer I decided to look for an aircraft of my own. With almost no money in the bank this was ridiculous but I looked anyway and found an advertisement in a flight magazine for 20 new Cornells, surplus air force trainers that had been repainted and reconfigured for civilian use. As the planes sold, and orders diminished, the price came down to a very reasonable $625 each.

It would not have occurred to me, but Dad suggested I approach the bank for a loan. Based on my enthusiasm and obvious determination to become a commercial pilot, the bank manager loaned me not only the Cornell's purchase price but enough to travel to Brandon, Manitoba, where the planes were located, and gas money for the flight home. I had a friend who decided he wanted one of the planes as well so we put in an order for two.

Dan McIvor, my flying instructor, and I then proceeded to Brandon. It was May, 1949. We flew with Air Canada in a plane similar to a DC 4 but with Merlin Vee 12s, the same engines used for the Lancaster bombers, instead of the Pratt & Whitneys used for the DC 4. In Brandon Dan made sure I was safe to fly one of the Cornells and then we started back to Vernon under clear blue skies with Dan in my friend's plane. I might have been safe to fly the plane but as things turned out, I definitely was not to be trusted as a navigator. I was used to flying in the mountains, with lots of landmarks. The prairies totally confused me. I put us on a course for Edmonton rather than Vernon and Dan, who was flying behind me, had to catch up and motion me – we didn't have radios – in the direction of

*An airborne Cornell PT26A, similar to the one Bill bought for $625 just after WW2.*
(Photo courtesy of the Canadian Museum of Flight, Langley, BC)

Kicking Horse Pass, far to the southwest. After that, I kept a much closer eye on my compass and started checking the place names on the sides of the grain elevators. This made it much easier to follow the aeronautical charts and we proceeded on to Vernon without incident.

Unfortunately, the Cornell was a very expensive plane to fly, so much so that I often took friends with me who would help with the fuel costs.

Even then, I only kept the plane for a year, but in that time I learned a lot about flying, especially when the other Cornell owner and I chased each other across the Okanagan skies.

I sold the Cornell for a bit of a profit and bought a Taylorcraft BC12D (CF-DRB) from Millard Air Services in Toronto in September, 1950. It was a high wing plane with a low drag airfoil which meant it went faster than other 65-horsepower aircraft. However, my return to Vernon was anything but speedy. First, I got weathered in at Toronto for a week, which cost me dearly in hotel and food bills. This was money I'd been planning to use for the trip home. Fortunately, the evening before I left, Carl Millard, from whom I bought the plane, treated me to a steak dinner, the last real meal I was to enjoy before arriving back in Vernon.

The trip home took 32 hours in the air over four days. En route I wondered constantly if I'd be able to stretch my few remaining dollars to pay for fuel. Then weather forced me down at the airport in Kenora, ON where I was temporarily distracted from my financial worries. I was on a long approach to the runway and equipped with a radio receiver but no transmitter, which meant I couldn't communicate with the control tower. I landed without incident and was rolling to a stop when a tremendous roar obliterated every other sound around me. I thought my new plane was self-destructing but then I saw a huge DC 3 go screaming right over top of me. Apparently I had taken too long in my landing and the bigger, and more to the point, faster plane had overtaken me. He had to repeat his approach and I figured I was in big trouble. But no. I was Number One on approach and, as I was soon informed, had the right of way.

My last stop before reaching home was in Castlegar. I had just enough money left to refuel but then I checked the oil. I was down a quart and short the 40 cents it would cost to top it up. Again, an air service operator came to my rescue, nourishing my plane this time rather than me. He told me the Taylorcraft wasn't going to fly without oil, poured in the required amount and told me to send him the money later. I made absolutely sure I did.

That same year, 1950, I started working in Kamloops as an apprentice air mechanic for Central BC Airways, the company started in Fort St.

James in the 1940s by Russ Baker. One of my jobs was sewing the fabric cover onto a Fairchild 71, a long, narrow aircraft with a 450 horsepower engine and nine-foot prop. There seemed to be miles of sewing, nine stitches to the inch, then a lock stitch. But, I figured, you can't know too much about aircraft maintenance. When the stitching was done, all of the seams had to be covered in two-inch wide tape and then the whole fabric cover was doped with an aluminum pigment and sanded and re-sanded to fill in the fabric weaves and bring up a smooth surface. Only then was the aircraft painted.

I kept my Taylorcraft at the Kamloops Airport and would fly home to Vernon every weekend, always conscious of my need to build airtime. One Sunday, as I returned to Kamloops, I realized just how much I needed the experience those 250 hours could afford me. The cross winds that day were much too strong for me to land safely on the runway. So I decided to land on a tie-down spot right in front of the main airport building where I would be flying into the wind instead of across it. It was almost a perfect plan. I was right over the tie down spot but hovering motionless and helpless in the wind, about 10 feet off the ground. Fortunately, our chief engineer happened to look out the window and see my predicament. He rushed to my rescue, grabbed one of the wing struts and pulled me down while preventing me from being blown backwards. Once the wheels were on terra firma, I jumped out and helped him with the tie down ropes.

I continued working in Kamloops, all the while building my hours and learning the engineering side of the airline business. By the time the ice was off the lakes in 1951, I had my commercial licence and was sent north to Burns Lake as a co-pilot with Central BC Airways. The company, which just two years later would become Pacific Western Airlines, needed pilots to supply the crews working on the new Kemano hydroelectric project that would produce power for the Alcan Aluminum Company smelter in Kitimat. The project involved construction of the Kenney Dam on the Nechako River and diversion of its headwaters, via a 10-mile-long tunnel through the Coast Mountains, to a power plant at Kemano, just off the Gardner Canal. Transmission lines carried the electricity 75 miles north to the Kitimat smelter.

In Burns Lake we had three German-made Junkers aircraft and a Norseman, all with 600 horsepower engines, and a 450 horsepower de Havilland Beaver, the first ever built. As there were no roads we flew everything – men, food, machinery, building supplies – to work camps on East and West Tahtsa lakes, about 85 miles southwest of Burns Lake, and the Kenney Dam to the southeast. This went on all summer and well into the fall. During the winter fewer flights were needed so I hired on with the survey crew as a rod man working out of the West Tahtsa camp.

Specifically, my job was to hold the measuring stick, or rod, for the engineer who used a transit to locate exactly where, on the face of the tunnel, the drillers should bore into the rock. I would then use paint

*The first de Havilland Beaver (CF – FHB) before it was painted.*

to mark the sites. Holes were drilled on three different levels and the explosive charges timed so that the centre area of rock would blow out first, allowing space for the upper level to drop and the lower level to rise. After the blast, the broken rock was removed from the tunnel via metal rail cars pulled by an electric-powered locomotive engine.

One night I had just finished painting the face and putting away the survey instruments when 10 tons of rock fell from the 25-foot high ceiling of the tunnel and smashed down onto the locomotive engine – the one I was just about to jump aboard and drive out of the tunnel. I didn't realize it at the time but that cave-in was a signal that my departure from

West Tahtsa was fast approaching. I stayed on for a few more months, working in the tunnel, which was now 3,000 feet long, and performing other camp duties such as snow ploughing, organizing the drillers to spend part of every day tramping down a landing strip for the few aircraft that did come in, and preparing diagrams of the tunnel as it progressed toward the coast.

*Building the tunnel through the coast mountains to the Kemano power station.*

Since starting the camp job I had kept my Taylorcraft at the lake. I used it for recreation and the camp manager was happy to have an emergency aircraft and pilot at the ready for the 200-plus camp employees. In January I decided to fly to Burns Lake for a bit of a break and met up with a buddy named Merv Hesse. Eventually Merv would learn to fly both fixed wing planes and helicopters and become part owner of Northern Mountain Airlines in Fort St. James, but in 1952 he was driving truck for a road construction crew. We did a few rounds of the town and ended up at the local skating rink where I spied a beautiful girl in a red jacket doing circuits of the rink.

"Who's that girl?" I asked Merv.

"You wanna meet her, eh?" he responded.

The girl's name was Antoinette (Toni) Wheeler and she lived a couple of miles out of town. Merv knew her because he gave her a ride to the high school every day. He introduced us, I borrowed a pair of skates and, having never skated before, made a fool of myself. But she didn't tell me to get lost.

I logged a lot of hours that winter flying to Burns Lake to see Toni. In May I quit at Tahtsa and got a couple of jobs in Burns Lake – one piling lumber and another working with a building contractor – so we could spend more time together. She finished school in June and we were married July 12, 1952 in Burns Lake with both families in attendance.

*Bill and Toni on their wedding day, July 12, 1952 in Burns Lake.*

In order to avoid any unwelcome visitors on our wedding night, I let it slip that we'd booked a motel room on Francois Lake, about 20 miles south of Burns Lake. Then, when the opportunity arose, we slipped away from our guests into the Burns Lake Hotel for the night. It was a nice piece of subterfuge – the would-be revellers all headed for Francois Lake when they noticed us missing – and just about the only one of my wedding schemes that worked.

My original plan called for a leisurely honeymoon flight down the coast to Vancouver using the Taylorcraft and a new set of floats. In order to pay for the floats, I sold my car. Then the floats arrived late and damaged so I had to buy back the car. However, the guy I sold it to had removed the engine and put it in another vehicle. That meant I had to buy a used engine from an auto-wrecker and install it in my old car. We left Burns Lake on July 13 and burned five gallons of aviation oil to Quesnel and another case of regular engine oil over the three days it took us to get from Quesnel to Vernon. By the time we reached Vancouver I'd burned through a second case of oil. This, of course, meant I was constantly changing filthy spark plugs. Fortunately, the used aircraft spark plugs I'd picked up from the base before we left Burns Lake fit the car engine.

And the motor was not the car's only weak point. The roof leaked too – all over Toni's new luggage. And, when I opened a bottle of Coke on the passenger door lock, I neglected to notice the bottle was pointed at Toni.

It took us six days in all to get to Vancouver but there was one bright moment. We were on the Hope-Princeton highway and passed a wreck in worse shape than ours. It had a Just Married sign in the rear window. That cheered us up a bit. Our first night in Richmond was spent at a hotel but neither of us slept well. The car doors wouldn't lock and everything we owned, except for the plane, was in the car.

The next day we found a basement suite and moved in. We cooked our first meal in the new place on a hot plate but when everything was ready we realized we had no cutlery. We ended up using popsicle sticks for spoons. The next day I saw an ad in The Vancouver Province offering a free set of cutlery with purchase of a year's subscription and I went for it.

With our domestic woes now well in hand it was time for me to get back into the flying business. The day after we rented the basement suite I was rehired by Central BC Airways to work in the company hangar at the Vancouver airport as an apprentice aircraft engineer. I retrieved the Taylorcraft from Burns Lake and, for a while, we used it to explore places like Pitt, Harrison and Cultus lakes near Vancouver and some of the lakes on Vancouver Island. Eventually, though, I decided to sell the plane and we put the money towards building a home in Richmond.

In the summer of 1953 I started flying solo as a commercial pilot. I had 375 hours under my belt and the company sent me to Powell River for three months where I flew an amphibious Seabee off Powell Lake, servicing logging camps to the north and south of that Sunshine Coast community. That fall our first child, Randal Stewart, was born.

*Bill and Toni with the Taylorcraft outside the Central BC Airways hangar in Vancouver.*

Unfortunately, I didn't make it home until two days after the birth and a short while later was sent north again, this time in a Travelair, to service the West Tahtsa and Kemano sites.

On most of these flights I was carrying little more than fresh food and the mail, but occasionally I carried more interesting cargo. About a week after one of my flights from West Tahtsa to Burns Lake someone – I can't remember who now – asked if I'd seen a gunny sack aboard the plane. I hadn't but proceeded to search the plane and found the bag stuffed under the pilot's seat where it had resided for a week. Inside was $4,000 in coins, the equivalent of about $40,000 today. I returned it to the rightful owners.

I logged about 150 hours on the Kemano project that fall then flew home to Vancouver for Christmas. Over the winter I earned my aircraft engineer's certificate which meant I was now qualified to both fly and fix the planes. It was a good combination because the company needed a pilot/engineer to start working out of Fort St. James. It was July 1954 and we – Toni, Randy, and I – were headed north as a family.

# Nipper

Since Fort St. James was a temporary posting for me, we set up house in the company office on the dock at Stuart Lake. There was a lot of water around but none of it running or hot. In order to wash Randy's diapers, Toni had to heat the water on a hot plate in the back of the building. Someone loaned us a boat so we could go to town for supplies. Since we had no fridge for perishables, I remember making quite a few trips. I flew a Cessna 180 for charter work that summer and a Fairchild 71 for the heavier work and I was busy flying the north country right up until December. But the real story of that time in Fort St. James was our reunion with Nipper, the half-Shepherd, half-Collie dog that became a bit of a legend in the Lakes District area.

Nipper and I first became partners when I was still living in Vernon. I got him when he was only a few days old from a guy who was giving puppies away at the entrance gate to a travelling circus show. I slipped him into my jacket pocket, with just his little head poking out, and took him home where I had to feed him every two hours. Like all pups, he was very playful and on the farm there were always lots of animal playmates. All went well until he set his eye on a batch of chicks as a new source of amusement. Unfortunately for little Nipper our "guard" cat had set herself up as chick protector and sent the dog sprawling as soon as he got close to the little fuzz balls.

"Never mind," says he, "it's planting time and there's lots of action over in the garden with all those hoes and rakes and seeds."

As you can imagine, he was not much help there so I carried him over to my jacket at the edge of the garden and told him to stay. Thinking this was a new game he followed me back into garden and waited for another free ride. I told him to stay put a second time with only marginally better results but he definitely got the message the third time. He didn't move again for the rest of the morning. Given that he was only six weeks old I considered this quite a feat.

*Bill and Nipper out hunting near Burns Lake.*

As Nipper grew physically, to about 35 pounds and 18 inches at maturity, so did his ability to learn. When I went swimming in Okanagan Lake he would jump off the dock from a four foot height and swim with me until he tired. And, just as I did, he would climb the vertical ladder, unassisted, back onto the dock.

In the fall I did a lot of pheasant hunting in the orchards around Vernon. Nipper was quick to notice I never shot the hens, only the cocks. He also noticed that in the confined spaces of an orchard a long range shot was out of the question and that, for best results, he had to flush the bird straight upwards on my side of the tree. Accordingly, he would scout ahead of me. If he detected hens, he would flush them and keep going. But if he detected a cock he waited for me to get into position and then flushed the bird. If I missed I got a dirty look. The one thing he never learned, or refused to learn, was to pick the birds up in his mouth. If I shot a pheasant he would stand over it until I arrived. If I shot a duck over water, he would swim to it then nudge it back to shore with his nose.

He also seemed to have a keen sense of danger. Whenever we went to the bush to cut trees for the tie mill, Nipper and Mom's dog, Smokey, would come with us. But as soon as we started cutting, Nipper would lead Smokey away from the fall zone and they wouldn't come back until all the trees were down. That's not to say he didn't have a bit of adventure in him. One of his favourite pastimes was to ride on my two-door Model A Ford. The two dogs would climb up between the fender and engine cowling, one on either side, and peer out over the headlights as we careened down the road at 30 miles an hour. They did, however, ride inside in rain or cold weather.

And, of course, he loved to fly. This was fortunate for him because I flew every chance I got en route to my recreational and commercial

*Nipper on West Tahtsa.*

licences. If I left him at home he would sulk until I returned. In 1951, when I transferred from Kamloops to Burns Lake, Nipper, who was now four years old, came with me. We stayed in a cabin on the lake and whenever I went out on a supply run Nipper would accompany me to the dock. If I left in one of the Junkers he would see me off and then head back to the cabin to await my return. If one of the other Junkers came back first he would ignore it. When he heard the machine I left in, he came down to the dock and everyone there knew I would arrive in a few minutes. The same held true if I left in the Beaver or the Norseman.

Whenever I traveled to Burns Lake to see Toni, Nipper displayed the dark side of his attachment to me. We often went for walks along the country roads and whenever we did, Nipper would come between us and try gently to separate our hands. I guess he figured if one companion was good enough for him, it should be good enough for me. It took a few weeks but Nipper eventually abandoned his divide and conquer routine and accepted Toni into the pack.

The initial trip out to Burns Lake had been in one of the Junkers. But I wanted my car handy, so the first chance I got Nipper and I hitched back to Kamloops in a company plane and I drove back to Burns Lake. Nipper had now covered the ground twice by air and once by road.

When Toni and I left Burns Lake that July after our wedding, we knew we were headed to Vancouver but we had no idea where we were going to live. As such we decided to leave Nipper with my folks in Vernon until we got established in the big city. About a month later I got a phone call from my mother saying that Nipper had disappeared. There were anxious hours and days of waiting but Nipper never came back. We had lost a good and faithful friend.

Two years passed, during which time I worked out of Vancouver, Stewart, Powell River, then back to Burns Lake before being posted to Fort St. James for the summer of 1954.

In the middle of August, Toni and Randy went into Burns Lake for a weekend visit with her parents. As I had a flight booked for Saturday I stayed home but would have Sunday off from work. Saturday night I went to the bar in Fort St. James and bumped into a fisheries officer who asked if I would help him with some work the next day at Pinchi Village, about 25 kilometres west on the north shore of the lake.

I agreed and he picked me up in his boat the next morning. During that trip I happened to mention Nipper and how I missed him. Well, someone must have been listening because as we approached Pinchi I saw a dog on the shore that looked so much like Nipper – dark fur, a little tan, some white spots – that my knees started to shake. Is it him? No, it couldn't be. Yes, yes – it is. Oh god, it is! He was weak and under nourished but it was unmistakeably him. I stepped on shore and we met for the first time in two years. The joy I felt was incredible, but how could he have gotten here? How could he have ended up here?

I will never know the details of that trip but I can only assume he walked, covering 700 miles and crossing three major rivers in just over a month. Later, I talked with my uncle, who lived near Hwy. 97 just north of Cache Creek, and he said he saw a dog that looked just like Nipper heading north on the road but paid it little mind because he didn't know the dog was missing. According to the building contractor I worked for in Burns Lake, Nipper showed up there mid-September, 1952. He recognized the dog but did not know where we had gone so took him to Babine Lake where he was building a fishing lodge. When work on the lodge was completed just before freeze up, one of the workers took Nipper over to Stuart Lake and he spent the winter moving between Pinchi and Fort St. James on the ice. When he was in the town he spent the nights in a garage near the school and the days playing with the children. He spent the summers in Pinchi, unable to move as easily between the two communities when there was no ice on the lake.

Eventually the Vanderhoof and Burns Lake papers published a version of Nipper's story. The Winnipeg Free Press even picked it up. I often think with sadness in my heart what Nipper must have felt when he reached Burns Lake to find we were not there. I would give anything to be able to trace his journey on a day to day basis. I do know he suffered a severe injury near the bottom of his rib cage at some point after leaving Vernon. The old wound was obvious when we were re-united and two years later, when we were living in Port Alberni on the west coast of

Vancouver Island, it started to fester. I took him to the nearest vet in Nanaimo and he lanced and drained the wound. But a week later it started festering again. I didn't have time for another trip to Nanaimo – it was several hours by road in those days – so I put Nipper in the bathtub and squeezed the infection out of the wound. While I was doing that I felt a hard lump under the skin. I used a razor blade to cut away the scar tissue and eventually removed a piece of sharp, burnt wood. After that I washed it, put in some cleansing powder and sewed it up.

Nipper never moved or whimpered through the whole procedure. Three days later I checked the wound site only to find Nipper had removed the stitches and licked the incision clean. It looked as if it had been healed for a couple of weeks. Some time later I had to use a toothbrush and peroxide to remove the scab which had formed over a still active ringworm infection on Nipper's nose. Once again, not a peep as I rubbed right down to raw flesh.

Nipper was with us for another nine years after the reunion at Pinchi. He became very protective of the children, displaying enormous amounts of patience as first Randy and then two more tykes, Gary and Lynn, tugged at his fur, sat on him and tripped over him as they learned to walk. And it wasn't only the children he protected.

On our way back to Vancouver from Fort St. James in the fall of 1954 we landed the Fairchild in Prince George. After a bit of exercise and some food and water I put Nipper into a company tool shed to spend the night and we went to a hotel. Given his habit of always guarding my airplanes, I should have realized he wouldn't still be in the tool shed in the morning. Instead he had taken up his sentry post on one of the Fairchild's floats, having jumped up on a convenient bench in the shed, removed a broken piece of glass from the window frame and jumped to the ground.

As devoted as he was to our family, Nipper did give himself about a week every year for romance. He was always exhausted on his return but recovered after a few days and resumed his usual role within the family. After one of these flings he returned, stayed home for a couple of days and then disappeared forever. We never saw him again. She must have been some girl, eh, Nipper?

Several years after my reunion with Nipper, the Fort St. James area was the site of another reunion. Over the years several pilots and more than one airline had been located here. In memory of its aviation history the community unveiled a scaled-down replica of a Junkers aircraft in a local park and invited several pilots who had flown in the area to the celebration. Fellow pilots, some of whom I hadn't seen for years, attended and we had a great time exchanging stories. One of those stories, perhaps the most amazing of all, belonged to Pat Carey, one of the first pilots to be hired by Russ Baker's Central BC Airways.

*Randy and Nipper resting.*

Carey had been flying an Otter for Pacific Western in the Stewart area at the head of the Portland Canal when he ran into a snowstorm. He lost all visibility and flew into the side of a cliff. The spot he hit was a wedge-shaped crack that stopped the aircraft dead and held onto the fuselage. He suffered facial injuries but was able to climb out onto a ledge and that's where he spent the night. He was rescued the next day by a helicopter using a long line. "If it had been 10 feet one way or the other, I would not be here," Carey said after his rescue. The aircraft just hung there for a few years and was eventually salvaged.

# Steak on a Shovel

Back in January, 1953, several years before Pat's crash and before I went to work in Powell River, the company sent me to Stewart. The first prospectors had come to the community in the late 1890s looking for silver and gold. They found it and, just before the First World War, the population had grown to 10,000. Since that time the town has had its up and downs. As I write this, the town is experiencing one of its down times with a population of fewer than 500 people.

I was to serve as helper, co-pilot and mechanic for a number of supply flights to the new Grand Duc gold mine at the head of the Salmon Glacier, about 30 miles north of Stewart in the same general area where an avalanche killed 26 miners in 1965. There were five of us in all – pilots Dan McIvor (my old flying instructor) and Harry Taylor, Wilfred Teece, Tom Clark and me. We flew north from Vancouver and after a stop in Prince George pushed on to the northwest through the Bear Pass and into Stewart. Today, as you drive through the pass, there is a beautiful lake at the toe of the Bear Glacier on the south side of the road. But in 1953 there was no road and the glacier flowed right across the pass and climbed the opposite slope.

At the mine site we tramped down a landing strip on an unnamed glacier just south of the Salmon Glacier and the mining crew erected their tents near the top of the strip. Later in the mine's development a bulldozer packed a nice, flat strip into the ice at the top of the Salmon

Glacier and this strip was used by a huge C-46 cargo plane that could carry 10 tons of freight. This plane eventually put us out of business, but initially our Junkers and the first Beaver ever made, CF-FHB, were the workhorses for the Grand Duc operation.

*A de Havilland Otter in good weather on the Salmon Glacier north of Stewart.*

Wind, varying visibility and other weather conditions always make mountain flying unpredictable and often hazardous. Further complications on this particular job included snow conditions on the glacier and the fact we always had to land uphill on a 15 degree slope. It is possible to land facing downhill but on skis you have no braking mechanism. If snow conditions are slick, you would just pick up speed as you headed downhill. On the other hand, if the snow is wet and sticky, it sometimes takes every bit of power you have to overcome the friction and get even an unloaded plane free of the ground. I have spent cold nights at inhospitable places when the aircraft just would not accelerate to take-off speeds.

For the first three days of the job the weather was with us and we were able to make several flights, hauling in food and equipment. Then we were grounded for three days due to heavy snowfall. There were already three feet of snow on the ground in Stewart and we got another three feet over those three days. This meant we had to pack the snow before takeoff and then we needed all 3,000 feet of runway to get the loaded planes into the air.

The Beaver carried about 1,000 pounds and the Junkers about 1,500. The weight of the cargo was limited by the amount of fuel we had to carry to ensure a round trip plus a good reserve to deal with unforeseen weather problems. On the morning after the heavy snow Dan McIvor took off from Stewart with the Beaver and proceeded to the glacier. The mining crew had packed the airstrip with their snowshoes, a big job since nine feet of new snow had fallen at the top of the glacier. Dan landed without incident.

A half hour later we had the Junkers loaded and Harry Taylor took off from Stewart. However, when he drew close to the landing strip, visibility was limited by low overcast. He was lined up with the strip and on his approach, but his depth perception was impaired by the overcast and the absolute lack of any contrasting dark objects like trees or rocks in the immediate vicinity. Adding to his confusion was a decay in the airspeed. He applied more power to keep the aircraft from stalling. He was still about a half mile from the airstrip and even with a wide open throttle it seemed he couldn't gain speed or, more importantly, altitude. This was likely due to the thinner air at higher altitudes and the heavy load. He could see the Beaver up ahead on the strip but he couldn't tell how far above the ground he was. That's when all vision through the windshield was obliterated as the propeller dug into the snow and threw it back onto the glass.

Acting quickly, Harry shut down the engine to avoid damage to the prop and prevent flying snow from being sucked into the carburetor and the engine. But he could do nothing to prevent the Junkers from sinking to its belly in the soft snow. Upslope, Dan McIvor had watched the whole thing and was already on the radio to Harry organizing a rescue operation.

Most northern pilots carry emergency supplies on all trips and Harry was no exception. He had snow shoes, sleeping bag, ration kit, shovel, blow pots to heat the engine, canvas engine tent and a rifle. He was loaded with food for the mining camp. What he didn't have was someone to help him dig the plane out of the snow.

Dan flew back to Stewart, informing the base of our predicament. Tom and I, who had stayed in Stewart to load the planes, gathered up extra sleeping bags and cold weather gear and were soon ready for the flight back to the head of the glacier. We landed about noon which gave us approximately three and a half hours to dig the Junkers out of the snow and move it uphill to the packed landing strip. Meanwhile Dan flew back to Stewart for another load of camp supplies, telling us to be at the glacier airstrip no later than 4:30 p.m. That would give us a half hour of daylight for the flight back to base.

*The Junkers (CF – ATF) mired in snow on an unnamed glacier near the Grand Duc mine.*

After snowshoeing to the Junkers we spent about three hours digging down to the skis and under the wings, then tramping out a runway. By 3:30 Harry started the Junkers' motor and after a warm up tried to move forward. Tom and I, one of us at each wing tip, rocked the machine in hopes we could get it moving. It wouldn't budge an inch. The grade was too steep and the snow under the skis too sticky. Also, it had been sitting too long and frost had built up on the bottom on the skis. We had jacks but no way to brace them in the soft snow and lift the aircraft to clean off the frost.

In our efforts to free the Junkers we lost track of time until we heard Dan approaching in the Beaver. We immediately headed uphill on our snowshoes towards the airstrip. Tired from our efforts to free the plane, Harry and I still made good time despite the steep grade. Tom fared less well and had covered only half the distance by the time we reached the Beaver. It was now 15 minutes past the time set by Dan for leaving the glacier and he wanted to take off immediately. Otherwise none of us would get back to Stewart. Somebody was going to have to stay with Tom – and I lost the coin toss.

Harry felt bad about leaving me there but a toss was a toss. I said good bye and started to walk back to the Junkers which was now just a dot in the fading light. It was a struggle trying to keep the plane in sight and stay on the trail. We fell, we stumbled and, worst of all, we worried we would miss the plane completely and have to spend a night out on the glacier with no food or shelter.

We made it but were now in total darkness. We rummaged around inside the plane until we found Harry's flashlight. The first order of business was supper and since Harry's plane was loaded with food for the camp, we had lots of choices. Perhaps foolishly we opted for steaks and were confronted immediately with the problem of how to cook them. No worries. We broke out the blow pots – torch-like devices used to warm up a plane's engine in below-freezing weather – and used a snow shovel as our frying pan. We cut the meat with a pocket knife, used our fingers for forks, ate bread and cookies for dessert, and boiled water for coffee in empty juice cans.

We were exhausted but sleep did not come easily that night. We were warm enough in our sleeping bags but we were on a very definite downhill incline and kept slipping to the rear of the aircraft. At one point I even tried jacking up the rear of the plane but nothing would hold in the soft snow. Adding to our unease was the weather; the wind blew and the snow fell all night long. By morning the plane was completely drifted in and we couldn't see the airstrip for blowing snow. We dared not move for fear of getting lost, so we fired up the blow pots again and had bacon, eggs and coffee for breakfast.

It continued to snow until mid-afternoon and then the skies cleared somewhat. That's when we heard the beautiful sound of the Beaver coming to our rescue. Not wanting to spend another night out on the ice,

*Loading the Junkers with freight for the Grand Duc mine.*

we hoofed it up to the airstrip where Dan was waiting for us with coffee, sandwiches and squares. We took off downwind and downhill and were back in Stewart in minutes, leaving the Junkers on the glacier.

And that's where it stayed for the better part of a week as weather prevented any further attempts to move it. Six days later all of us flew back to the site in the Beaver. This time Dan taxied us downhill to the Junkers. We immediately set about turning the Beaver uphill for takeoff into a strong wind. We tied a rope to the tail of the plane and started tugging it around in the deep snow. When we had it at right angles to the wind, Dan applied full power to the engine in an effort to help us turn the plane ... but we lost our grip on the rope and Dan went hurtling across the glacier, spewing so much snow we couldn't see the plane. And then suddenly we couldn't hear it either, just the wind blowing over the glacier.

When things cleared a bit and we moved forward in the wake of the plane, we realized he had dropped into a wide ravine on the glacier. Just as we reached the edge of the ravine we first saw, and then heard, him climbing upward on the far side of the hollow, the rope still attached to the tail ski and flapping in the wind as he turned the Beaver for Stewart.

With the added manpower and colder weather, which firmed up the snow, we managed to get the Junkers back up to the airstrip that day and sooner than anticipated. As we sat drinking coffee in the mining camp cook tent, waiting for Dan, we decided most of our crew would fly back to Stewart in the Beaver and I would return with Harry in the Junkers.

When Dan arrived he figured an uphill takeoff into the wind with the load of men would be impossible so he opted for the downhill route. The wind was gusty and blowing downhill at about 20 miles an hour as he gained enough speed for lift off. That's when the plane slowed suddenly, the tail lifted and the Beaver came to rest standing on its nose. The engine was buried in the deep snow and the tail was almost 30 feet in the air. The drag of the skis, the weight and pull of the engine, the downhill slope and a gust of wind at the tail all contributed to the mishap. As he felt the plane getting away from him, Dan had cut the power which prevented damage to the prop but that, and the fact no one was seriously injured, were the only good things about this situation.

The crew literally fell out of the airplane and Wilf and I did a quick check for damage. Aside from a broken radio and one ski cable, there was none. Better yet, the rope was still tied to the tail. Everyone took a handful but when we started to pull the plane down, the rope broke. We got another rope and after several attempts one cowboy succeeded in lassoing the tail. Some more rope tugging and digging got the plane back into a horizontal, take-off position but it was now too dark for the flight to Stewart.

We spent that night confined in the mining camp tents and were greeted next morning by snow and mist which kept us grounded until 4 p.m. when the skies cleared somewhat. It was decided Dan and Wilfred

Teece would leave first. Harry and the rest of us would leave 15 minutes later in the Junkers if weather hadn't forced the Beaver back to the glacier airstrip. And that's just how it played out. Dan left and 15 minutes later we followed. But when we landed at Stewart there was no sign of the Beaver and no one at the base had heard from Dan or heard the aircraft pass overhead.

It was now dark, our other plane was missing and we all had dread in our hearts. Harry spent most of the night organizing a search for the morning while the rest of us lay awake trying not to imagine what might have happened.

We had perfectly clear skies next morning. Hugh Russell, who flew with Central BC Airways out of Burns Lake, left home very early and flew directly over the mountains to Stewart. Our plan was to use the Junkers to scour the terrain between the glacier airstrip and Stewart while Hugh was to follow Dan's flight path and carry on past Stewart in a southerly direction. Another plane, from the company base in Prince George, was scheduled to join us later in the morning.

That plane was never needed. Hugh found Dan and Wilfred perched on another glacier south of Stewart. They had been unable to find a way down through the clouds onto the Stewart airstrip and ran so low on fuel and light that Dan had to put the plane down. Hugh siphoned some fuel from his plane into the Beaver and both planes flew back to Stewart. The search was called off at 10 a.m. and the Prince George plane diverted back to its base.

To celebrate the safe return of our friends we all went across the border to Hyder, Alaska that night for some high flying of a different kind. There is a ritual there called "getting Hyderized" which involves 190 proof Everclear moonshine and I was well and truly initiated. It was three days before I could keep a cup of coffee down.

Later that month the Beaver sustained damage to the tail which we couldn't repair as it involved major structural work. We took the plane apart and had it barged back to the company hangar in Vancouver. When we dismantled the ventral fin we found a large X painted onto the skin, denoting FHB's earlier experimental status. This was the first Beaver and the one used for flight testing prior to civil use. The ventral fin had been added to this plane after testing to increase stability and became a feature on all future Beavers. Usually the X is removed when the plane is sold after flight testing. In this case it had been hidden by the addition of the ventral fin. If only I'd had a camera ….

The X was not the only anomaly associated with FHB. When the maintenance crew tried to reassemble the plane with new parts they wouldn't fit. It had been hand built in the factory and was a bit shorter than the production models. The crew had to hand make replacement skins for the tail section. I last flew FHB in 1962. It now sits proudly in the Museum of Flight in Ottawa and is in good company. The very Junkers we used at the Grand Duc mine so many years ago – CF-ATF – sits there with it.

Weather, snow conditions, heavy loads and darkness had contributed to our woes in Stewart. None of those conditions was present when, at Fort St. James in the summer of 1954, I had to do an emergency landing with our ancient Fairchild 71. It all started with a phone call from a local prospector who wanted to do some survey work just east of the community. There were three of us in the plane – myself, the prospector and Jim Henry, the town's postmaster, who came along for the ride. I circled the area at about 800 feet for half an hour at reduced throttle and a lower-than-usual airspeed while the prospector and Jim did some mapping and photography. When they finished, I throttled up for cruise power and started for home.

It started with a bit of a clatter and before I could read the instruments and diagnose the problem, let alone come up with a plan, the engine seized and the prop stopped dead. In an instant we had attained glider status, the only sound that of the wind over the wings, and we were headed down.

I had two options for a landing site – into the trees or onto a swamp just to my right. The swamp was shaped like a bowling pin with shallow, muddy water in the larger or bottom part and deeper water through the narrows in the upper part. But the narrows looked a bit too narrow to fly through so I opted to land in the shallows.

I did wonder if the mud would bring us to an abrupt halt but I didn't wonder for very long. It only took about 40 seconds to lose 800 feet and then we were down and unharmed. I had two paddles on the plane and it took us a half hour to push ourselves forward, bit by bit, through what is referred to in aviation lingo as loon shit, to the shore of the lake. My radio call was answered by our Terrace base and pilot Doug Chappel flew out with a Junkers to see if he could help. We knew there was no way he could land in the swamp so we started to walk the eight miles back to Fort St. James along the old McLeod Lake Trail. Doug did manage to spot us and land on a lake near the trail. But we missed him and ended up walking the whole distance back to the town. Doug waited an hour then took off, saw that we were okay and headed back to Terrace.

Now we had to rescue the Fairchild. The Vancouver office sent me an engineer, Greg Temperly, and a replacement engine which I ferried to the site – along with tools, food and camping supplies – with the help of a crew of local Indians, a team of horses and a wagon. We cut down some trees in the narrows, to make room for the plane to pass into the deeper water, and then towed it through to our camp with the help of a small, aluminum boat. I did try, unsuccessfully, to dam up the lake's outlet in hopes of raising the water level. We nosed the plane up onto the shore and then built an A-frame we could use to winch out the old engine and put the new one in. In a properly equipped hangar, the job would have taken just a few hours. Out there, in the heat, black flies and mosquitoes, where if you didn't have the right wrench you had to make do without, it took us four days. When it was done we put in fresh oil, fired it up, let it run for a good long while and then shut it down.

There were no oil leaks or any other obvious problems. Just about this time, and for the first time since our predicament began, a nice wind came up, blowing about 20 miles an hour right through the narrows and onto the nose of the plane. I told the engineer to button up the engine cowling. I was leaving immediately.

The takeoff through the narrows and shallow water went much better than I expected. The wind really helped and the muck under the floats put the aircraft on the step rapidly as the water compressed on acceleration. I landed at our dock on Stuart Lake a few minutes later and exactly one week after the engine failure. The crew got back the next day and told me the wind had died down about 15 minutes after I took off. To this day I wonder if I could have made it without that wind.

The old engine was beyond repair with a broken crankcase but it could have been worse. In most engine failures the propeller will windmill until the aircraft is on the ground. In this case it had seized solid. When a propeller stops suddenly there is always a major break in the crankcase or crank shaft. If the crankshaft breaks at the main bearing, the prop departs the aircraft and a weight and balance problem ensues as you've lost about 200 pounds from the nose. This causes the tail to drop and all of a sudden you need a lot more airspeed to maintain control ... and a much longer body of water.

This was the only total engine failure I experienced in the course of 17,000 hours of flying. I've had other engine problems but was able to fly to a base or a lake for repairs. To some extent I credit the quality of the Pratt and Whitney engines with my ability to avoid any truly disastrous accidents. It wasn't by chance they were selected as the engine of choice for trainers, fighters and light bombers during World War Two.

There is an epilogue to the engine failure incident. It all started several years later when Pacific Western was hired to fly a group of well-heeled dignitaries around the north in search of investment opportunities. Some of these gentlemen were from Great Britain and were accompanied by a British Broadcasting Corporation (BBC) reporter with a tape recorder.

On Day 2 of the visit some of them, including the reporter, got weathered in at Fort St. James. I wasn't there but some of the pilots started telling stories about northern bush flying and, of course, the tale of my impromptu landing with the Fairchild came up. As the day wore on, and the bar opened, the tales got taller and taller and the reporter's tape recorder kept on running. By the end of the evening I was being referred to as Wild Bill Lopaschuk.

Eventually an edited version of the recorded material found its way onto BBC Radio and the reporter decided it would be a good idea to create a contest for school children. The contest, which called for the kids to write a ballad about Wild Bill, the Canadian bush pilot, was advertised on the BBC and drew more than 100 entries. Here's a couple of verses from one of them:

*The engine roared through the desolate bush;*
*The animals cowered in fear;*
*The aircraft it raced across the lake*
*And gracefully rose up into the clear air, clear air,*
*Gracefully rose up into the clear air.*

*Back to Prince George Bill Lopaschuk flew,*
*His heart was full of good cheer;*
*He'd saved the comp'ny a thousand-score dollars*
*And come back to his wife and two children so dear, so dear,*
*He'd come back to his wife and two children so dear.*

A few years later, one of the British dignitaries was back in the north and made a point of meeting the legendary Wild Bill. Instead of some eccentric character with a long beard and all decked out in buckskins, he found me seated at a desk, dressed in my Pacific Western uniform, writing in my log books. What a disappointment.

In addition to that short stint of fame on British radio, I also garnered some time in the spotlight demonstrating what not to do as a fly fisherman on the Ted Peck fishing show, a weekly, 1960s TV program from Vancouver. I flew Peck and his crew on three occasions and on our last trip together the cameraman was getting footage of proper casting technique. Unfortunately, when his camera settled on me, my fly line got hung up in a tree behind me. This clip was used at the beginning of the show, in the middle, and there was Lopey, still caught in the tree, to close out the program. Had I ever gotten another chance to fly those guys, I think I would have given them a rough ride in retaliation for their on-air pranks.

# Cat's Paws, Sharks and Trumpeter Swans

In January 1955 we moved to Port Alberni which was to be our home for the next two and a half years. The city is at the head of the 25-mile-long Alberni Inlet, formerly known as the Alberni Canal, on Vancouver Island and about 50 miles west of Nanaimo. It is one of BC's largest ports and, during the time we were there, a major forest industry community. It is also an excellent place, especially during the winter, to take a crash course, figuratively speaking, in foul weather flying.

In windy conditions, which account for most of the time on the coast, flying is done at about 50 to 75 feet above sea level. Pilots do this to avoid downdrafts. If, for instance, a loaded Norseman aircraft, which will carry 10 people or a ton of freight, got caught in a downdraft at 500 feet, it would hit the water. There would not be enough power to overcome the sink. The air in one of these downdrafts descends at a great velocity. As it nears the water, and cannot descend anymore, it reverses in a great, gusty circle of upward moving air from sea level to 100 feet. These cat's paws, as they're called, are rough but flyable, which is why we fly low in windy conditions. Sometimes I have had to fly so low along the shoreline that the spray from waves smashing into the rocks has washed over my plane. And one time the headwind was so strong at Estevan Point on the

Hesquiat Peninsula I spent about 15 minutes looking at the lighthouse. My ground speed was about 10 miles an hour.

Fog was another challenge, even in the summer. It could be perfectly clear inland and when we hit the coast we'd have to find our way either under or around the fog banks that blew in from the ocean at zero to 100 feet above sea level. On one trip, with nine passengers on board, I was communicating on the radio with Bill Harvie, another Pacific Western pilot, about the bad weather spilling into the Alberni Canal. Bill had a full load too and we were both headed back to base. We knew we were close to each other and I figured I was in the rear as we headed up the canal. I put up with the weather for awhile and then decided to land and wait it out. Just as I touched down on the water there was a tremendous roar about five feet above me as Bill passed overhead. He had decided to land too and, with the lousy weather and the limited forward vision in a Norseman, had not seen me at all. They don't come much closer than that.

Of less importance than visibility, but always annoying, was the dramatic temperature change associated with the fog. The Norseman was a very hot aircraft with no insulation on the firewall between the bulkhead and the cabin. On sunny summer days the sweat would be pouring off us as we ducked under a fog bank into the cold. When we jumped out to dock the plane we were instantly chilled.

Most of my air time in Port Alberni was spent ferrying loggers to and from such places as Sarita River, Bamfield, Kennedy Lake, Ucluelet, Tofino, Thasis, Gold River, Zeballos and numerous un-named locations. These trips averaged about eight minutes, which was another reason we didn't bother climbing to higher altitudes. The company had five pilots and we flew a fleet of five Norsemen, a couple of Beavers, a Cessna 180 and a stagger-wing Beechcraft. The Norseman was the workhorse as it carried the most people and handled the ocean swells the best.

All the aircraft were located at Sproat Lake where we had a dock, ramp, shop and fuel facilities. Each morning we would ferry whatever aircraft were needed for the day to our office at the docks on the Alberni Canal at the end of the town's main street. We'd pick up our passengers there, then proceed with the scheduled runs to various places either inland or along the coast.

*A Norseman with some of the PWA crew at Port Alberni. Jim Lightbown is on the right in the front row.*

The pilots were Jack and Gordon Moul, Jim Lightbown, Bill Harvie, Bill Smith, and me, Bill Lopaschuk. The engineer's were Bill Hendrick, Al Warner, Bruce Apps, and John Hunt. That's a lot of Bills so we let the engineer keep his name and renamed the pilots Harvie, Smith and … Lopaschuk? Nope, that wouldn't work. In the end I was renamed Lopey and that's how I was known for the rest of my aviation career. I mention this because one Monday morning, before we agreed on the name changes, a reporter showed up on the dock looking for a story. We were taking loggers back to their camp on the Sarita River near Bamfield and I was loaded and just pushing away from the dock when the reporter arrived. I shook his hand, told him I was Bill Lopaschuk and suggested he talk to Bill Harvie, the next pilot in our line up at the dock. They introduced themselves and the reporter got the same song and dance. Sorry, gotta go! Check the next pilot. By now the reporter was more than a little miffed but thought he'd give it one more try.

"So," he says to the third pilot, flippantly, "I suppose you're Bill Smith or something?"

"That's right," said Bill. "How can I help you?"

We were a tight-knit, fun-loving group and sometimes got up to a bit of mischief. One morning we decided to give the town a thrill and do a five-Norseman take-off right over our downtown office. Once we were loaded we taxied out into the harbour, pointed our noses into the wind, advanced throttles and lifted off all together a few hundred yards from town. We were 100 feet off the water, the 600 horsepower engines all screaming, when we turned over the office and headed to our various destinations, leaving the dispatchers to handle the dozens of irate phone calls from Port Alberni residents. Management advised us later our stunt was definitely an unacceptable way to advertise Pacific Western's service.

*Wearing PWA's less than ideal uniform in Port Alberni.*

Another of our favourite pastimes was complaining about our uniforms – navy hat, pants, tie and jacket and a white shirt. This was a smart-looking and practical uniform for the big, passenger plane captains who never had to go outside. For the west coast, it was silly. The horizontal rain and salt slime meant we were often soaked through and our wives spent endless hours washing and ironing our work clothes. With three kids, two of them still in diapers, Toni didn't need the extra laundry.

The company hats were a damn nuisance too. There was no good place to hang them in the aircraft cabin and our head phones wouldn't fit over the top of them. My solution to the problem was to stick my head out the window. Good bye hat. Unfortunately a new one was always issued.

Eventually, the Pacific Western managers heard us and we got khaki pants and a leather jacket. This gave some protection to the upper body and I wore eight-inch-high Wellingtons when docking on some lonely beaches. The boots were especially nice when I had to move the plane two or three times to avoid being grounded on the beach by a receding tide.

One of my more pleasant assignments in Port Alberni was flying salesmen to the various communities along the west coast of the island. It was pleasant for a couple of reasons. First, I got to fly the Beechcraft 17, a sleek, fighter-like, bi-plane that could reach 145 miles an hour on floats. It could do 200 miles an hour on wheels but I never got to experience that. Nonetheless, even on floats, takeoffs were exhilarating. Jack Moul also liked to fly the Beechcraft. He was a Second World War pilot and said the Beech reminded him of flying a Spitfire. The second reason I enjoyed these trips had to do with the people and hospitality we encountered as we hopped from community to community all the way north to the tip of the island. A milk salesman and a tobacco company representative used to team up and twice a year we'd spend three days finding out who made the best coffee and cookies along the coast. While the salesmen spent about an hour getting their milk and cigarette orders, I'd get the community gossip and share news from the outside world with the locals.

Medical evacuations were another part of the job and not all of them ended well. On one occasion I was dispatched to Chamiss Bay on Kyuquot Sound to pick up a logger who had sustained a crush injury to one leg. It took an hour after I landed for the stretcher to arrive and in that time bad weather had started to move in. I took off for Port Alberni anyway, but after an hour in the air, rain, mist and excessive winds forced me to abandon that plan. I landed instead at Esperanza where at least there was a health post staffed by a doctor and a nurse. As we tilted the canvas stretcher to get it off the plane, a large pool of blood spilled out. The man was bleeding to death.

Blood was ordered from the hospital in Port Alberni and an attempt was made to fly it to Esperanza, but weather and then darkness put a halt to that effort. The pilot was Bill Smith, a very capable foul weather flyer, but there was no way he could get through. The poor chap died from loss of blood at eight o'clock that night, despite the doctor's best efforts to stop the bleeding.

*Bill Smith, another of the Port Alberni pilots.*

On another trip, this time to Vancouver, I was transporting a boy who had suffered a head injury. He had been comatose at the Port Alberni hospital for a week and it was decided to send him to a higher level of care. I was flying the stagger wing Beechcraft and a doctor was attending to the boy in the back of the plane. An ambulance was waiting for us at the airport in Vancouver. The trip takes about 45 minutes and after about 30 minutes in the air the doctor tapped me on the shoulder and said there was no rush. The child had died. I felt badly and always wondered if the boy might have lived had he been transferred sooner.

One of the saddest coastal incidents I was ever involved with was the loss of six passengers headed for Kemano in early January, 1953. PWA pilot Jimmy Siddle, flying a Grumman Goose, ran into a blinding snow storm in a channel near Butedale on the Inside Passage. He had no room to turn the plane so he decided to put it down in the channel. According to reports of the incident the plane hit something in the water, most likely a log, and the Goose flipped upside down. Siddle managed to get all six of his passengers into life jackets and out a door in the rear of the plane that was not yet underwater.

For a while they clung to the aircraft. It was being carried by the tide and was slowly sinking into the channel. When they passed a point of land about 150 yards away they all decided to swim for shore through the 36-degree (F) water. Siddle, a former long-distance swimmer, was the only one to make it.

By the time we were told Siddle's plane was missing, it was too dark to start the search. We left first thing the next day. I was a spotter in a Beaver piloted by my old flying instructor, Dan McIvor, and PWA's Jim Dunbar was flying a second Beaver. We battled the weather all day and sometime in the late afternoon we managed to get past Butedale. Jim Dunbar spotted Siddle first. He was sitting on a rocky ledge about four feet wide and had been there for more than 24 hours, unable to move because of the steepness of the cliff.

McIvor landed and taxied as close to the ledge as he could, then shut off the engine. I got out onto a float and paddled the Beaver close enough to the ledge that I could pluck the hypothermic Siddle off the rock and bundle him through the side door of the Beaver. I was then able to paddle us far enough away from the cliff that Dan could start up the engine. From there it was a short hop back to the health post at Butedale where Siddle got the medical attention he needed. He later said he counted more than 20 boats going by in the channel during his ordeal but they were all closed up against the weather and the people on board never saw him.

On a more pleasant note, another of my jobs for a couple of years was to fly grain to Lonesome Lake near Bella Coola for Ralph Edwards' trumpeter swans. Edwards had acquired land on the lake in 1912 which he developed into a farm. He married Ethel Hober in 1923 and they had three children. Together they spent years caring for the swans that wintered on the lake. Trumpeter swans are the largest water fowl species in North America and, prized for their skins, had been all but wiped out by the 1930s. Conservation work, including that done by the Edwards family, is credited with their continued existence.

My part in the Lonesome Lake operation involved picking up the grain from a barge at Bella Coola and making four trips, taking about one ton each time, up to the farm. I always enjoyed my visits with Ralph – I'd first met him in Vancouver when, at the age of 65, he was getting his pilot's licence – but was always frustrated because I could never get close to the swans. Wary of strangers, they would swim out into the middle of the lake when anyone other than Ralph and his daughter Trudy approached.

Ralph did start to build his own airplane but eventually bought a Taylorcraft on floats and used it to commute between Bella Coola and Lonesome Lake. In 1966 he left the farm and took up commercial fishing at Oona River on Porcher Island. The story of Ralph's family and their work with the swans is told in a book by Leland Stowe entitled *Crusoe of Lonesome Lake*.

As I mentioned earlier, one of our frequent stops when flying out of Port Alberni was at Sarita near Bamfield on Trevor Channel. It was also a favourite breeding site for basking sharks. Each spring these huge animals would come to the Sarita River and swim in the sound just off the docks where we loaded our passengers. On one trip I'd finished loading and was trying to find a pathway through these 30-foot-long, four-ton monsters. They have two fins on their backs, the larger being the front one, so I could tell the direction of travel.

As soon as I saw an opening between them I accelerated for lift-off and was almost off the water when a huge shark surfaced crossways right in front of me. The floats hit the back of the shark, the impact bouncing me into the air. I had enough airspeed to keep on flying but knew the floats had sustained damage. Instead of landing at our office at the foot of Port Alberni's main drag, I landed on Sproat Lake right near the ramp and repair shop. The passengers took a taxi to town and we spent three days fixing the floats.

Another vivid memory from my time in Port Alberni, and one that carried far less risk, at least to me and my passenger, involved a charter to Nitinat Lake just down the coast from Bamfield. I had landed on the lake and was reading while waiting for my customer to finish some business.

*Gary, Lynn and Randy in the early years.*

That's when I heard the sound of an outboard motor. When I looked up I saw a dugout canoe churning upriver towards me at about 25 miles an hour, the 20 horsepower outboard running wide open. I knew the coastal Indians were good with boats but I had never seen anything like this. The boat's sole occupant was standing up on the gunwales at the front of the canoe, hands in his back pockets, enjoying the breeze. Crazy, I thought, but impressive.

Toni and I will always have fond memories of Port Alberni. For one thing our second and third children were born there – Gary David, June 4, 1955 and Lynn Catherine, June 6, 1956. I'd missed Randy's birth in Vancouver, due to weather and work in Powell River, and dads were not allowed to be present when Gary was born. But then the rules changed and I was allowed into the delivery room for Lynn's arrival.

And we had great times with the other members of the Pacific Western crew and their families. In the end it was the weather that convinced us to leave. I remember one three-week period in winter when it snowed lightly every day and the fog blanketing the town never lifted. After work one day I packed Toni and the kids into the car and drove them to a forestry lookout just above the town. As we basked in the sunshine we could hear dogs barking and cars moving just below us but we could see nothing but the fog. After three winters I'd had enough and looked for a posting back in the north.

*Bill holding daughter Lynn outside their home in Port Alberni.*

# Prospecting From On High

We moved to Prince George in May of 1957, a time of great prosperity and growth for BC's northern capital. The Hart Highway (Hwy. 97) now connected the city to the Lower Mainland in the south and Dawson Creek to the north. BC Rail, then known as The Pacific Great Eastern, was extended to Prince George from Quesnel. The forest industry was already well established in the community and provided a platform for the emerging pulp and paper industry.

It was now mining's turn. About the same time I was preparing to leave Port Alberni, Pacific Western got a contract to survey the mineral potential of all northern BC, from Babine Lake north to the Yukon and from the coast to the Alberta border. We called it the Wenner-Gren survey after the Swedish entrepreneur, Axel Wenner-Gren, who had cooked up a major northern development package with the W.A.C. Bennett government. Many of the projects in the deal never materialized but a couple did – the Williston Reservoir and the mineral survey.

The airline assigned me to the survey and, off and on for the next three years, it provided me with some of the toughest flying I have ever done. But before I got started on the survey I needed to get my family into a house. We soon discovered that we'd come to town at the wrong time. With rampant economic growth comes a huge demand on housing. All we could find on short notice was a very old house with a pronounced tilt. One corner was about six inches off level – a great place to locate lost marbles. We put in a year there and then bought some property at the bottom of Peden Hill near where the Costco store now sits. My carpenter dad helped me frame in a new house and we moved in as soon as it was wired, plumbed and had windows. I scrambled that fall insulating the place and putting up Gyproc, usually at night long after the kids had gone to bed. We did manage to get the place liveable that winter, with the addition of an oil heater and a fireplace, and then spent the next 11 years there.

*Randy, Bill, Lynn and Gary at home in Prince George.*

I remember at one stage in the early phases of construction I needed help pouring concrete. Ordinarily, hiring help would not have been a problem but this particular summer was a bad one for forest fires and every available man had been scooped up by the government to battle the blazes. Even the regulars at the local taverns had been pressed into service. However, a friend of Toni's knew three guys who were lying low, just under the BC Forest Service radar. I hired them for a day to pour cement and then went off to work myself, flying the fires with a Forest Service observer.

Later that day the observer, George Flieger, who wanted to see how work on the house was progressing, drove me home in his well-marked Forest Service vehicle. When we pulled up to the house it was as if we'd tossed a fox into the hen house. My workers spotted the vehicle and scattered, thinking they would be eating smoke before the sun went down. Eventually we finished the house and, since it was right across the road from a school, that's where the kids received a good portion of their education.

Meanwhile, back to the Wenner-Gren survey. The whole point of that exercise was to map the mineral potential of northern British Columbia. The maps would be made available to the mining industry, which, in turn, would use the information to further investigate potential ore bodies and develop working mines.

For me, it meant flying exactly 250 feet off the ground in straight lines, three miles apart, for eight to 10 hours a day for three years. Several instruments, including a magnetometer and a scintillation spectrometer, were mounted in a rack on the floor behind me. They measured magnetic fields, radioactivity and other wavelengths emanating from the earth's crust and spewed out paper tracings as I flew the grid lines. If we hit a hot spot the flight lines would be reduced to a separation of only 100 feet. Since the instruments were most accurate at the 250-foot level, it meant we had to maintain that elevation as we flew from peak to peak across valleys in a kind of concave, saucer-shaped trajectory. If any area was missed because the angle was too steep, we flew it again from a better

*Maintaining 250 feet down a steep slope during the mineral survey.*

direction. In this way we never left a gap in charting the whole northern half of the province. Most days we flew from five a.m. to 10 a.m. and again from 5 p.m. until dusk, thereby avoiding the turbulence caused by the mid-day heat. Rainy, foggy and windy days were spent maintaining the plane or reading. It was just too dangerous to fly in bad weather at 250 feet.

Another challenge, given the number of hours we were in the air everyday, was to keep track of the fuel. I had six fuel tanks but only three of them had gauges. That meant I had to keep close track of time when using the tanks without gauges. If I miscalculated, ran out of fuel and the engine started to sputter, I would lose 200 feet of altitude before I could get the next tank to kick in. That's okay when you're at 8,000 feet but at 250 feet I would have been shaving the tops off the trees.

All of the flying was done in a Beaver (CF-ICL) on floats. Our campsites, which included fuel caches, were at Finlay Forks, Telegraph Creek, and Weissener, Thutade, Dease, Coldfish, and Damdochax lakes. We also had fuel caches at Spinnell and Eddontenajon lakes. Fuel deliveries were made with a Stranraer flying boat, a huge double-wing plane with two 1,500 horsepower engines mounted on the top wing. This aircraft was capable of carrying fourteen 45-gallon drums at a time. It

*CF-ICL on the beach at Coldfish Lake.*

was a very sad day later in the survey when the Stranraer crashed on a salvage mission and all three men aboard were killed. The plane had been scheduled to fly north from Prince George but weather forced a delay. The pilot, Bill Cooper, decided he could put the time to good use by flying south with a couple of helpers, fellow pilot Ian Watt and an engineer, to a small lake near Quesnel. A Beaver had crashed there a few years earlier and the plane's floats had never been picked up.

They landed without incident, found the floats and tied them to the back of the Stranraer and tried to take off. The plane never came off the water. Instead, it cut a swath through the trees and burst into flames when the fuel tanks ruptured. Inspectors later confirmed the tied-down floats on the back of the plane had disturbed the air flow over the tail. Elevator control was lost and the plane crashed. We heard about the loss on the company radio and flew south as soon as weather permitted to pay our respects to the three families.

We worked with a crew of seven to eight men on the mineral survey – myself as pilot/engineer, an aircraft maintenance man, a mineral exploration chief and his second-in-command, a cook and two or three

*A Stranraer flying boat, similar to the one in which pilots Bill Cooper and Ian Watt died.*

prospectors who would do on-the-ground assessments of mineral hotspots identified from the air.

We went through three cooks in our first year. The first was an alcoholic who quit when the booze ran out. The second believed breakfast was at seven a.m. and supper at six p.m. If we wanted to eat at some other time, we were on our own. I fired him one night when we got back at seven o'clock and he told us he'd thrown our supper out because we were an hour late. The third cook appointed himself our moral guardian and put saltpetre in our food to discourage any inappropriate thoughts involving women. The fourth was the answer to our prayers – a wise and hard working Chinese man who kept a spotless cook tent and baked excellent pies and cakes. We were all quite saddened when, in our second year of operation, he died. It was only after his passing that we discovered he was 95 years old. We never found as good a cook during the remainder of the project.

*Crew members in camp during the Wenner-Gren survey.*

Our first camp was at Finlay Forks and is memorable to me for two reasons. The first reason is that it no longer exists, lost forever beneath the waters of the Williston Reservoir. But when we were there it was the site where the Omineca, Finlay and Parsnip rivers all joined the Peace

River and flowed as one through a gap in the mountains en route to the Arctic Ocean. Finlay Forks was also the site of an old trading post run by Roy McDougall and his wife, Marge. Roy had come into the country in 1925 and the store, located on the Finlay just before it entered the Peace, was a place where travellers had always been able to count on a good meal and a place to sleep. We stayed in cabins there and thoroughly enjoyed the hospitality lavished on us by these pioneers of the Rocky Mountain Trench.

*The survey crew on the Finlay River. Roy McDougall, centre with pipe and hat, operated the trading post at Finlay Forks.*

Flying at 250 feet all the time made it much easier to spot wildlife. I once flew over a sow grizzly that had just made a kill in a meadow and was so engrossed in eating that she paid little attention to the plane. This was not true of her cubs. As the Beaver approached they took off at full speed in opposite directions. Then they seemed to realize, in unison, they had put too much distance between themselves and their protector. As if directed by some comic choreographer, each cub turned at exactly the same time and hot-footed it back to mama.

On another day we were flying just above tree line when we started across a clearing and a huge grizzly boar seemed to reach up in fury and try to claw us out of the sky. I was grateful we didn't have to land anywhere nearby. I'm sure that bear would have hunted us down.

*Get it together boys! Nipper tries to straighten out the crew.*

In addition to laying the groundwork for the mineral development of northern BC, the Wenner-Gren survey was responsible for a major change to the de Havilland Beaver. At that time the plane came from the factory with an eight foot, six inch prop. Given the difficult ascents and descents called for on this job, I wanted a prop that would give me more agility in the mountains. I'd flown a Fairchild 71 which had the same engine as the Beaver but turned a nine foot prop so I requested the same for the Beaver. It took a few phone calls and a lot of letter writing by our Vancouver engineers, and some test flying and paper work by me, but eventually we got the Beaver certified for the longer blade. It made a huge improvement but there were times when I wished for a lot more horses out in front of me, especially when we flew up blind canyons that did not show on the charts. At 250 feet it was very difficult to see all of the as yet uncharted corners and grades until you were upon them. I eventually learned it was safer to fly down these canyons than climb blindly up them. I also learned not to trust the maps.

There were times too when we had doubts about the geological instrumentation aboard the Beaver. One day we were cruising down a valley when the radioactivity tracings started running off the scale. After about 10 minutes of this we headed for home. The spectrometer was obviously malfunctioning and the readings were useless. But as we got closer to base camp the readings started to stabilize and eventually returned to normal. We did a thorough check of the instrument and could find no fault and when we re-flew the canyon the instrument behaved normally. All of this

*Merv Hesse brings Toni into Thutade Lake for our fifth anniversary.*

took place about two weeks after the USA had conducted nuclear bomb tests in the South Pacific. Had we flown through a pocket of radioactive fall out?

It was not only the terrain and our instruments that provided surprises on the Wenner-Gren job. In July of 1957 we were just about to move camp from Thutade Lake, just east of what is now Tatlatui Park, to Cold Fish Lake in what later became Spatsizi Plateau Wilderness Park. As we prepared to leave, a Junkers flew over and then landed on the lake. I was surprised to see my buddy Merv Hesse climb out of the pilot's seat but even more surprised when his passenger emerged. It was July 12 and Toni had decided she was not going to spend our fifth anniversary alone.

I was ill-prepared for the big event. We were moving camp, it was cold and rainy, I had only one sleeping bag and a little pup tent but, worst of all, I hadn't had a bath in two weeks. I remember the lake water was freezing – it had snowed in the area just a few nights before – but this was a special occasion and I had to be presentable. We delayed our move to Cold Fish and that night Toni and I made do with my sleeping bag and a light one she'd brought along. It was an anniversary we'll always remember.

After setting up our new camp the next day at Coldfish, we headed back to Prince George for a few days of rest and to pick up supplies. Toni and Merv had flown from Fort St. James so I had to drop her there to pick up her car. The wind was howling, making it too rough to land on the lake, so I put the Beaver down on the Stuart River. But there was no dock on the river so I hailed a fellow with a boat who came out to the plane to collect my wife. I dropped her suitcase into the boat, she hunkered down against the wind and spray, and I lifted off for Prince George. I still get static over that part of the anniversary.

Our fourth camp that year was at Weissener Lake, perched high up on the east slope of the trench. We stayed there from the late summer

*Pilot Ian Watt, later killed in the Stranraer crash, helps Margaret Bourke-White ashore at Weissener Lake.*

until freeze-up, enjoying a magnificent setting where you could be flying at 200 feet and then the ground would drop 4,000 feet to a valley bottom. In the early fall there would often be fog on the lake in the mornings, delaying our takeoff until about 10 a.m. I used the time to take pictures of the yellows, oranges and reds of fall. At night the skies were filled with the shimmering lights of aurora borealis and their sound reminded me of tinkling ice crystals on a freezing lake.

It was during our time at Weissener Lake that we played host to Margaret Bourke-White, a world-renowned photographer from Life magazine. Ian Watt, who later died in the Stranraer crash, was using a Beaver to fly Margaret to various locations for a photo feature she was doing on northern BC. They stayed with us for three days and I can remember she always had trouble with her arthritic hands in the early morning cold. She had also been diagnosed with Parkinson's disease in 1952. To help her we would load film into her cameras before she took off for the day with Ian. Earlier in her life Margaret had been on assignment throughout Europe and spent time with Mahatma Gandhi in India. She was the photographer who took the famous photograph of him sitting on a carpet near his spinning wheel shortly before he was assassinated.

*Weissener Lake*

The final two camps we used during the Wenner-Gren survey – Damdochax Lake and Dease Lake – had both played prominent roles in the history of northern BC. Damdochax Lake was on the old Telegraph Trail that had served as both a communications and transportation corridor in the north up until the 1950s. However, by the time we arrived, the trail's main users were animals. Because it was the flattest spot on the lakeshore, the mechanic and I set up our tent right on the pathway. Three nights later a wolf pack walked down the trail. We would not have known until morning save for the fact the alpha male sat 10 feet from my tent and, in the dead of night, howled for all he was worth. The whole camp was immediately awake but it wasn't until first light that we realized the pack had walked right through the kitchen tent and past our garbage pit and meat cache without touching a thing. This respect for property did not hold true for a grizzly that made a weekend visit to the same camp while we were in Prince George. Anything that was to his liking he ate, or at least sampled, including 24 quart cans of engine oil that were punctured and drained. I could only guess at how poorly the bear felt after that meal. But there was no doubt about the huge mess we had to clean up when we returned from town.

We also had two-legged visitors at Damdochax. One afternoon a father and his two sons hiked into our camp en route to Telegraph Creek. They looked like they could use a break. They said they'd started out with two pack horses but ran out of food and had to kill one of the horses. They dried the meat, hoping it would last through the rest of the journey. It didn't and they were again out of food when they reached us. They stayed with us for two days and we advised them against the completion of the journey. The trail was badly overgrown and there was little or no browse for the remaining horse. But they were determined to make it so we gave them a good supply of food and wished them well.

Damdochax was also the site of another little wrinkle in our daily routines. We got trapped there for three days, grounded by smoke from nine different forest fires in the area. I had reported the fires to the Forest Service but they were so busy in the south they had to ignore these northern blazes. It was bad enough not being able to fly but the worst part was knowing the fires could come tearing through our camp at any time. We had a ramshackle raft tied up to the shore, plus the Beaver, and planned to climb aboard and get to the middle of the lake if the flames closed in. Fortunately, the wind shifted and moved the fires away.

Dease Lake, our other historically important camp, figured prominently as a Hudson Bay Company fort and a gold rush town in the late 1800s and a marshalling site for materiel used to build the Alaska Highway in the 1940s. Road building machines, men and supplies were hauled by steamboat up the Stikine River to Telegraph Creek. From here they were transferred to metal land barges and pulled cross country by bulldozers 70 miles to Dease Lake where they were again transferred, this time onto floating barges, for the final leg of the journey down the lake. From the lake they moved into the Dease River, then to the Liard River, and finally to Lower Post on the path of the new highway. We saw several of these now-rotting barges during our time on the lake.

During the gold rush days thousands of prospectors and miners had called the north end of the lake home. By the late 1950s there wasn't much left but we did see evidence of a hand-built, eight-mile long canal running northeast from Little Dease Lake into the main lake. The miners used the canal to separate gravel from gold in their sluice boxes.

Given the consistently difficult flying conditions associated with the Wenner-Gren survey – low altitude, 10 hours a day in the air, blind canyons and more – I'm always impressed with the fact we managed to complete the whole thing. At one point I'd given us only a five or 10 per cent chance of actually finishing. But it wasn't the day-to-day grind that almost ended it. It was a routine, weekend flight home from Dease Lake to Prince George at 8,000 feet. We had enjoyed smooth air and calm wind conditions since takeoff and were approaching a mountain in the Sustut River area when we hit a shear wind. All hell and a lot of other things broke loose.

The left wing dropped and we started to roll upside down. That's when training and experience really kick in. "Fly the airplane," I kept saying to myself. "Fly the airplane." Had the right wing dropped we would have ploughed into the face of the mountain. We were semi-inverted, gaining airspeed and plunging down toward the river when I finally managed to get the left wing up, bring the nose back to level and resume normal airspeed. We hadn't crashed but it was still a miracle no one had been injured. A tool box that had been sitting on the floor between the rear seats had rocketed upward and dented the ceiling. Maps were strewn all over the cabin and a set of knives we were taking to Prince George for sharpening were now on the floor after flying around the cabin during our plunge. We had dropped 2,000 feet and my heart was still racing. But I did offer up a prayer of thanks that everyone had fastened their seatbelts.

*Sheer power and ground effect were often all that saved us in blind canyons.*

A Beaver on floats is not an aerobatic aircraft so I was seriously worried the struts and wings may have sustained damage due to the shock load they'd experienced. And the headwinds and rough air currents we fought for the rest of the trip did nothing to relieve my anxiety. But when the engineers back in Prince George gave the plane a clean bill of health we realized the de Havilland designers had done a very good job with the Beaver.

# Flying the Snow Pack

Another part of the Wenner-Gren/BC government development plan for northern British Columbia involved a major hydroelectric dam on the Peace River. The W.A.C. Bennett Dam was built by BC Hydro between 1962 and 1967 about 14 miles west of Hudson's Hope, flooding the Finlay and Parsnip River valleys and creating the almost 1800-square-kilometre Williston Reservoir. In 1980 the Peace Canyon Dam was built 14 miles downstream and, up until 2000, these two structures supplied about one third of BC's hydro electricity.

Pacific Western got involved in the project in a few ways – escorting potential investors to survey possible dam sites, flying men, supplies and equipment to the site once it was chosen, and doing regular measurements of the snow pack at 12 high-elevation lakes feeding into the reservoir area.

My first experience with the project was in 1959 when the airline was hired to fly potential project investors to the Peace River area. These were very influential people, both Canadian and foreign, representing large amounts of money. In my group of five there was a Canadian senator and two members of the British House of Lords. One was Lord Polwarth, a former governor of The Bank of Scotland, and the other was the 2nd Lord Tweedsmuir. He was the first son of Sir John Buchan, a former Governor-General of Canada, a well-known author and the man after whom BC's Tweedsmuir Park is named.

As pilots for the expedition, Bill Harvie, from Port Alberni days, and I were instructed to show our esteemed guests the entire watershed, including two possible dam sites, one at Finlay Forks and the other just above the Parley Pas Rapids on the Peace River west of Hudson's Hope.

My first stop was the potential dam site above the rapids. Actually, the rapids were more like a waterfall with a 10-foot drop. We landed on the river and tied up to the shore about a mile above the rapids in fairly fast water. Solid rock walls on either side of the river would provide the kind of stability the dam engineers wanted, especially in the event of an earthquake. Our plan was to spend an hour or so examining one side and then taxi across the river to have a look at the other side.

I had tied a rope to the front strut of the Beaver, and when it was time to cross I asked a helper to hold us with the rope until I got the engine going. I could then drag the rope as we crossed the river and retrieve it on the far shore. I loaded the passengers then climbed in through the left door, not noticing that my shore helper had moved forward and was now standing ahead of the floats. When I fired up the engine the prop caught the rope, whipped it out of my helper's hands, jammed it behind the prop hub and stopped the engine. We started to drift downriver towards the rapids just at the edge of the fast current.

This was hardly a scenario to inspire investor confidence. But luck was with me. I was able to lay my hands on another rope immediately and throw it to my on-shore helper. At almost the same time the shore-side float hung up on a very conveniently placed rock. The Parley Pas Rapids would not get us that day. It took me about 20 minutes of hard work to cut the first rope loose and we then managed the crossing without further trouble.

We spent the remaining time before noon looking at the other possible dam site and then landed on a mountain lake where Bill Harvie and his group of moneymen were to join us for lunch. I lay down on the shore of the lake while some members of my group tried, without success, to land a few fish. It was a hot day so I guess they weren't biting. That's when my investor group came up with an alternate plan. They all stripped and leapt off my floats into the lake for a cooling swim. When

Bill's group arrive they joined right in. Ten lords a' leaping and neither Bill nor I had a camera.

During our stop at the lake, Lord Tweedsmuir, whose name was John Norman Stuart Buchan, marvelled at the size of the conifer trees in the area and wished out loud he had some seedlings he could take back to England. I later sent him a packet of seeds from the Forest Service and a month later received a letter from The House of Lords thanking me. He died at a cottage in North Berwick, Scotland in 1996. I never found out if he planted the seeds.

When the Bennett Dam was eventually built on the Peace just west of Hudson's Hope, the engineer in me really enjoyed watching the progress of this multi-year undertaking. The first phase involved drilling a series of tunnels through the rock wall on the south side of the river to divert the water. Then the base of the dam was laid down on the dry river bed. A tunnel, stretching from one side of the canyon to the other, was constructed beneath the base to allow for monitoring of any leakage from the dam.

*Diverting the Peace River for construction of the W.A.C. Bennett Dam.*

The dam itself was constructed with gravel from a moraine about four miles east of the actual dam site and transported via a five-foot wide conveyor belt. The belt, which curved upward at the edges to contain the rock, also drove a generator which created enough electricity to power the rock crusher, provide lighting and run a few pieces of stationary equipment. In this way machines and men could work around the clock.

The crusher ground the rock into seven different sizes. The fine crush was placed in the center of the dam and the coarser grades were placed successively to the outside. The river, when restored to its original path, would carry fine silt into the coarse outer layers of the dam and eventually create an impermeable barrier. Any leaks could be detected from the tunnel below.

My second experience with the Williston project – flying men and supplies into the dam site – was fairly routine but did provide one humorous episode when the BC Hydro brass decided they wanted to save money by cutting the amount of flying time. The corporate solution was to move our base of operations north from Prince George to McLeod Lake, about 75 miles closer to the dam site on the Peace River.

Unfortunately, it was a warm winter and the ice on McLeod Lake was not strong enough to support the move. But the phones would ring and I would promise each time to check the ice again once we got a good cold spell. We never got the cold spell but the Hydro executives kept calling. Finally, after a month, they decided to come north and check things out for themselves.

I drove six power company executives to McLeod Lake, and we walked out onto the ice. There were a few suspicious humps here and there so I poked a shovel into one and almost fell into the open water underneath. I decided right then we would not be landing our aircraft on the lake.

Despite this rather obvious sign, one of the company men asked me how much weight I thought the ice would support. Since all six of them were standing apart from me in a tight little cluster, I suggested 1,200 pounds was about the limit in any one place. It took a few seconds for my reply to register and then they scrambled for shore.

We never did get colder weather that winter and continued to fly from Prince George. Even if the lake had been safe, any money BC Hydro might have saved in fewer flying hours would have been spent building a whole new operations base with office facilities, crew quarters, tool shed, kitchen, power and fuel sources, and lighted repair facilities for the planes. It would have taken months of planning and construction.

In addition to our supply runs, we were also hired to do the flying for a snow pack survey at 12 sites above what would eventually become the Williston Reservoir. The sites on either side of the Rocky Mountain Trench were chosen for their proximity to lakes where we could land. All were at an elevation of 4,000 or more feet, roughly 50 miles apart, and formed part of the Peace River watershed. By cataloguing the snow pack every year, and the plan was to do it for 10 years or more, Hydro officials

*CF-ICL on the ice at Finlay Forks.*

would get a good idea of how much water they could count on from the spring runoff and how much they would need to hold in reserve to ensure a constant power supply for the province.

We flew into each of the lakes in the fall and put a long stake into a marshy area adjacent to the lake. The stakes were flagged, so we could find them again after freeze-up, and served as a guide when the snow pack measurements were taken. Each location was visited once a month from January through March and twice in April.

The surveyors taking the measurements used six-foot long, hollow, aluminum tubes that screwed together and could reach a depth of 30 feet. Prior to each measurement the rod was weighed and then cored down through the snow until it picked up a plug of moss. This would ensure it was at ground level. It was then removed, weighed again – weight giving an indication of water content – and the depth level marked on the outside. The first measurement would be taken a foot from the flagged stake, the second at the two-foot mark and so on. This would ensure the same core hole didn't get used twice, guaranteeing a perfect sample with each measurement. We also had to be careful not to compress the sampling area with our snowshoes.

*Bill measuring the snowpack above the Williston Reservoir.*

As always snow conditions presented a challenge. The hard, slippery stuff was good but soft or gravel-like snow could seriously lengthen our planned three-day circuit of the lakes. In soft snow many, many hours were spent packing a track with our snowshoes in front of each of the aircraft's skis. After a couple of years of this I asked for wider skis and, as with the longer propeller, there were several hoops that needed jumping through. But in the end our new skis were about 30 per cent bigger and floated higher on the snow, significantly reducing the amount of snowshoe work.

Weight and thinner air at the elevation of the lakes also complicated takeoffs. When the surveyors said they needed another man to help with the measurements I groaned. Another body with sleeping bag, cold weather gear and food would mean an extra 300 pounds and make getting airborne even harder. So I volunteered to do the work myself. It saved on the weight and gave me a way to keep warm while the plane was idle.

I didn't have such a good solution, however, when Hydro bosses from Vancouver decided they'd like to come along sight-seeing on our snow pack flights. On one occasion, when it felt like I had the entire head office staff on board, I was able to provide them with a novel experience. The plan was to survey four lakes and then take the lot of them to Fort Ware at the junction of the Finlay and Kwadacha rivers for the night.

Fredrikson Lake, just east of Thutade Lake, was our fourth stop. It was late afternoon, the snow on the lake was soft and there was more of it falling. Those snow conditions combined with a full load meant the plane would not accelerate to takeoff speed. And it was too late in the day to split the load and make two trips to Fort Ware. So Hydro's finest dined that night on canned beans and coffee heated on an open fire and slept in summer sleeping bags on a tarp as the snow fell softly – and melted – on top of them. It was a soggy, chilled and chastened bunch of sightseers that arrived at Fort Ware the next day.

Even without a plane full of BC Hydro officials, there were occasions, mostly weather related, when we had to spend a night out on one of the lakes. If there were just two of us, we could off load all the equipment from the Beaver and sleep in the back. It was inconvenient but doable. But one winter I started negotiating for more. By summer I had talked our crew chief into putting up some shelters on a few of the lakes. We built pre-fab A-frames at six of the lakes and a Pan Abode cabin at Trygve Lake, our most northern snow pack stop in what is now Tatlatui Provincial Park.

At my suggestion Pacific Western hired my two sons, Randy and Gary, to help with construction, and Toni to cook for us. Lynn, our daughter, missed the week long paid vacation as she was at a summer figure-skating school in Edmonton. We trucked the buildings up to Uslika Lake, about 135 miles northwest of Fort St. James. From there we flew one shelter a day into the lakes and made two trips for the Pan Abode. The de Havilland Otter was the perfect plane for our work as it could carry one of the A-frames, the four-person crew and all of our equipment and food.

*One of our A-frames in the mountains above the Williston Reservoir.*

In subsequent years we, and many other travellers, made good use of these buildings. I remember one trip in particular. It was April 18, my birthday, and the crew chief and I got weathered into one of the lakes. We tried from noon until dusk to fly out of the valley but snow showers blocked our way every time. When we had resigned ourselves to not getting home, I commented that it was a lousy night for a birthday party. The crew chief then asked how I knew it was his birthday. Our mood lightened after that as we shared not only the same birth date but a small libation, a fried steak and, of course, our conveniently located shelter.

Unfortunately, the cabin at Trygve Lake was demolished, the victim of a Parks Branch management plan that rejected such structures. Given the number of times people have used remote cabins like the one at Trygve to escape severe weather conditions, I take exception to some bureaucrat in a nice, warm, Victoria office dictating their removal. As a commercial pilot flying regularly in northern BC, and sometimes in less than ideal conditions, I knew where every one of the old cabins was and considered them a kind of lifeline when the weather got bad.

I doubt very much that any Parks Branch manager ever had to prepare an aircraft for a night on a remote, high elevation lake at 30 or 40 below zero and then get it running again the next morning. It would take 45 minutes in the bone-numbing cold to drain the engine oil, being careful not to contaminate it, remove the battery, jack up the skis so they wouldn't freeze to the surface of the lake, and put a tent over the engine. But once that was done we could retreat to the safety of cabins like the one at Trygve where it was possible to keep the battery and engine oil warm for morning, prepare a meal, melt snow for drinking and sleep in comfort. I don't like to think of the alternative and it's a sure thing the people responsible for the removal of the Trygve cabin never did.

*Working a remote fuel cache.*

The Williston project taught me a lot about flying in adverse winter weather and one of the important lessons learned was to avoid fuel-wasting side trips. There were gas caches in the north but who wanted to dig down through six to 20 feet of snow to get at the barrels? We made all our fuel stops at places like Germansen Landing, Fort Ware and Finlay Forks where the fuel drums were protected in sheds and could be moved on sleds to the aircraft, where there was coffee, hot food, a bed when needed and friendly people eager for news from the outside. Those same people – people like Roy McDougall at Finlay Forks, Wes and Maggie Westfall at Germansen Landing and a First Nations woman named Teresa at Fort Ware – would also radio us crucial weather and temperature reports when we were trying to decide whether or not to leave Prince George. Teresa worked for the store keeper in Fort Ware and eventually moved to Prince George, went to nursing school and ended up working at Prince George Regional Hospital.

But sometimes, even when you're warm, well rested, well fed and the weather is good, you can get blind-sided and that's exactly what happened one frigid morning just after I took off from Finlay Forks for Prince George. It was minus 38 C and I had spent two hours warming up the Beaver. I ran the plane over the snow for a while to wear the frost off

*Roy McDougall (centre) and trapper Ed Stranberg on the Finlay.*

the bottom of the skis and then took off into a clear sky with just a thin wisp of cloud at the 1,000 foot level. All was well until I hit that innocent, little ribbon of cloud. That's when the windshield, the side windows and all of my instruments completely frosted over and I lost all contact with the outside world. This is not good when your elevation is only 1,000 feet and there are hills all around. I had no idea as to my airspeed, if I was upside down or right side up, or where I was in relation to the hills.

I tried to open a side window but it was frozen shut. So I did the next best thing. I took the comb – there were no credit cards in those days – out of my pocket and started scraping the frost off my side window and the glass covers on a few of my instruments. That's when I discovered the temperature had risen from minus 38 C on the ground to above freezing at the 1,000 foot level. And because it takes a while for a mass of glass and metal to warm up, the warmer, moister air in the cabin had frozen to the cold glass surfaces of my plane, cutting me off from all visual references. The ice soon melted in the warmer air and I tucked another "lesson learned" into my log book.

As if I didn't already know that ice and airplanes could be a bad combination, it was reinforced on a trip to the east of Great Bear Lake one fall. The weather was freezing when I landed on a good sized lake to pick up some prospectors. It was so cold that as soon as I landed, the float rudders froze and would not drop into the water. This meant I wouldn't be able to steer out of the wind and into the shore.

Unwisely, as it turned out, I left the engine at idle speed and stepped down onto one of the floats, intending to kick the rudders down. My feet no sooner hit the icy float than I was on my backside with my feet in the water on either side of the float and I was slipping down the float towards total immersion. Luckily, there was a bollard on the float, a post we used to tie the plane to a dock, and it stopped me from going into the frigid lake. I was on the offshore side of the aircraft so if I had gone in, the moving plane would have left me stranded in the middle of the lake.

Another reminder to stay on guard, even in good weather, came on a flight from Fort Nelson to Prince George. Falling ice crystals had forced me to overnight in Fort Nelson but the weather cleared enough for takeoff by morning. The temperature was about minus 25 C on the ground and visibility improving all the time. About 40 minutes into the flight, and at an altitude of 4,000 feet in calm air, I noticed the visibility improving even more. That's when I hit what felt like a brick wall. In fact, it was a 40 mile-per-hour head wind. When I looked out the side window I could actually see warm air rising over the colder air, like heat rising

*Bill digging CF-ICL out of the snow on Tudyah Lake, north of Prince George.*

off hot pavement. When I looked at the temperature gauge it read plus 10 C. Trying to buck the head wind and cope with the turbulence meant I wouldn't have enough fuel to reach Prince George so I detoured to Hudson's Hope. The detour delayed me to a point where it was too late to try for Prince George so I spent a second night away from home.

I know there are those who were saddened by the damming of the Peace River and creation of the Williston Reservoir. But that project was miniscule compared to another water diversion project dreamed up by engineers south of the border. My part in that undertaking occurred when I was asked to fly four Americans around northern BC. We were flying at about 4,000 feet but I had no idea what my passengers were looking for. So I asked, with the intention of making their time in the air as meaningful as possible. Their answer appalled me.

Essentially, they were surveying the land with an eye to creating a water diversion project that would have turned an enormous part of the province into a reservoir. Developed during the 1950s and 60s, the North American Water and Power Alliance (NAWAPA) was a series of plans calling for dams to be built in Alaska and the Yukon, trapping the waters from a drainage area of 1.3 million square miles. A huge portion of that water would then be channelled into a 500-mile-long, man-modified section of the southern Rocky Mountain Trench. It was to be 10 miles across and 300 feet deep throughout its length.

Such was the scope of the project it called for a canal 30 feet wide to be constructed from the reservoir across Canada to Lake Superior. Ultimately the canal would be widened and extended to the west so that Great Lakes freighters could sail from the Gulf of St. Lawrence across the prairies and into Howe Sound north of Vancouver. Other phases of the project called for water from the reservoir to be delivered to water-poor areas of Canada, the US and even Mexico. It sounds preposterous but in 1964 an American west coast engineering firm actually delivered a developed NAWAPA plan to a sub-committee of the US Senate. It called for 369 separate projects. Needless to say it never got built but one wonders if it isn't still percolating in some American minds every time we hear about water shortages south of the 49th parallel.

# Treasures From Heaven

Back in the 1950s and early 60s a regular part of any bush pilot's workload involved air drops – food, tools, machine parts, almost anything – from the belly of a low flying aircraft. When I worked for Pacific Western in Prince George we had a contract with the BC Forest Service for this work. Many of our flights were to supply fire-fighting crews in remote parts of the province.

Whatever was needed was packed into boxes supplied by the Forest Service. Each package weighed about 40 pounds which was the maximum our parachutes could handle. The parachutes were eight feet in diameter and attached to the packages. On a signal from the pilot an observer in the back of the plane would drop the package through a hatch specially constructed to prevent the accidental loss of observers and/or packages. When the package had dropped about 15 feet, static cords attached to the plane would open the chute. The best altitude for air drops was about 100 feet; it gave the chute time to slow the package before it hit the ground and was low enough, in theory, to prevent any significant wind drift. Accuracy was critical, especially in areas with trees or swamps nearby.

Whenever there was a major fire in a remote site inaccessible by road or lake, ground crews hiked into the area and the fire boss would select a suitable drop site, often an open grassy or marshy area. When I arrived I would make a pass or two over the site, checking the wind condition and the length of the drop site. The air observer would then harness up and position himself over the hatch, ready to drop the most important items first. If we missed the middle of the drop site on our first run, corrections were made on the second run.

*Bill and Merv Hesse with Bill's three children.*

I flew the aircraft at about 70 miles an hour or 90 feet per second. If the drop site was 450 to 500 feet long we could sometimes drop two packages in one pass. But it was crucial that someone on the ground watched the drops. Five hundred feet is a big separation and packages got lost if not tracked right to the ground, especially in marshy areas. Heavy items like shovels, axes and pulaskis (a special firefighting tool that combined an axe and a mattock in one head) were dropped at a very low altitude without a parachute. In this way they would hit the ground while travelling horizontally and be easier to find. An axe can go deep into swampy ground when it lands vertically.

For the most part we used de Havilland Beavers and Otters for this work and I have made up to 200 drops in a day. The little bubble Bell helicopters were available but couldn't handle the major quantities of freight needed to fight a big fire. They were good for five-minute return trips up a mountain slope and they were also used to return parachutes to the base camps where chute packers were hired specifically for this work.

Of course, as one might imagine, not every drop was perfect. I once

*A de Havilland Otter at PWA's float plane dock on the Fraser River in Prince George.*

had to deliver bedding, equipment and food to an initial attack crew camped on a bank of the Quesnel River. It was late evening so I dropped the sleeping bags on the first run followed by a bunch of equipment on the next two passes. On my last run the chute billowed out and then seemed to float forever, landing – where else? – on the opposite side of the river. One member of the ground crew actually swam the river and retrieved the food package.

Another incident, this time involving one of my fellow pilots, could easily have ended in disaster. After every drop the observer hauls the static lines back into the aircraft. On this particular occasion one of the lines swung back and got stuck in the horizontal stabilizer on the tail of the plane. The observer tugged on it, trying to get it free. This had a dramatic effect on the attitude of the plane. The pilot immediately tried to correct the situation with his control column. The two of them were having a tug-of-war while the plane roller-coastered through the air. It would have been funny had they not been flying at only 100 feet above ground level. Eventually the observer realized what was happening and stopped tugging. And, at our request, the Forest Service shortened the static cords so they would no longer reach the stabilizer.

Some drops, on the other hand, worked out exceedingly well. I was once dispatched to drop a radio at a Forest Service fire lookout. The lookout, naturally enough, was right on the top of a mountain with steep slopes descending from the peak. A miss of even 20 feet could put the package far down the mountainside. There was a stiff breeze so I had to come into the wind and judge the drop time of the chute so it wouldn't drift off the drop site and down the mountain. Also, I thought, a good updraft and the package would float forever. I calculated as best I could and then signalled for the observer to make the drop. It seemed to hang in the air for an awfully long time but eventually settled to the ground, right at the feet of the control tower operator. He hooked up the radio quickly and thanked us as we headed back to base.

Another time I was sent to drop some medicine at a cabin on the Torpy River, about 65 miles east of Prince George. One member of a group that had travelled up the river by boat had slipped near the cabin and aggravated an old back injury. He needed a special medication to control the pain and had none with him. About 15 minutes into the flight I asked the observer about the weight of the box as it had looked very light when loaded aboard the plane. There was nothing in it but a few pills and that would make for a problematic chute opening. There were no lakes handy, where I could pick up a few rocks to give the package some heft, so a seat cushion and a crescent wrench from the plane went into the box.

Our next problem was the drop site. The Torpy River ran on one side of the cabin and a forest hemmed it in on the other side. There was, however, a small garden patch the size of a six by six foot ground sheet near the cabin. That would have to be our target. We made three passes of the site, to get the feel of the terrain and check wind conditions – it was dead calm – and on the fourth pass we dropped the package. I banked quickly to get a look and watched as the box dropped into the garden. Bull's-eye!

Much of the credit for those successful air drops belonged to the observer in the back of the plane. He would have to watch for the pilot's drop signal then look down through the open hatch as he dropped the package. Then, as the plane banked into a three- or four-G turn, he would have to keep himself anchored while retrieving the static lines and getting the next package ready for exit. On any given trip we could make 15 to 20 passes. I sometimes wondered how those guys ever held onto their lunch.

The other big job we did for the Forest Service was water bombing. We used an Otter equipped with a 200 gallon tank. The tank was mounted inside the aircraft and could be removed easily when not in use. The Canso flying boat, which could drop 600 gallons, was available in British Columbia but was stationed wherever the fire potential was highest. This was usually in the south and, since it could take hours to get this plane up north, we used the Otter for rapid response work.

Travelling at 60 to 65 miles an hour, we could fill the tank in about 15 seconds. This would use up very little distance which meant we could load using relatively small lakes close to any fire. The actual release took three seconds and the water would cover an area about 100 feet long by 75 feet across. It was perfect for a lightening strike or a small fire. It also made for a bumpy ride. When you drop 200 gallons of water, which weighs about one ton, in just three seconds, the plane rises about 20 feet, all on its own.

On normal supply flights we carried an air observer who recorded all of the action and manned the radio. But insurance regulations prohibited us from carrying any Forest Service employees when we were water bombing so the pilot made all of the decisions about how best to wage the airborne war against the flames.

One Saturday afternoon while I was barbecuing steaks at home in Prince George, I got called out to a fire just north of Quesnel near Ten Mile Lake. I hurried to the float dock on the Fraser River, near where Ft. George Park is now located, picked up a load of water on takeoff and soon spotted the smoke in the distance. Just as I approached, the blaze crowned and started moving through the tree tops. I dropped my water and knocked the flames down but I'd need a fast turn around time if I was to keep them from spreading.

I had two choices for loading – the Fraser River or Ten Mile Lake. I chose the lake as it was about 200 feet higher than the river. The only problem with the lake was boaters. It was Saturday afternoon and there were lots of them but I figured they would stay out of my way once I picked up the first load. And they did, for the most part. But there was one boat with three guys on board that decided it would be fun to race along beside me as I picked up each load. And each time, the boat got a little closer to the plane.

After dumping about six loads on the fire in rapid succession, each time having to dodge the idiot boaters, I'd had enough. The fire would need a few more loads but the urgency had eased off. I came in for the next load but instead of heading for the fire I dropped 200 gallons of water from about 20 feet on my tormentors. It was a direct hit. As I turned for another pick up I saw two of them in the water and the third guy trying to get the motor started. They did not try pacing me after that and, contrary to my expectations, they never phoned either the Forest Service or Pacific Western to complain. I would have just said I had to jettison my load in order to avoid a collision.

As part of Pacific Western's contract with the Forest Service we were often sent out after a lightning storm to spot and hit any fires that might have started. With six hours of fuel on board we could do an extensive search. On one of these occasions I was sent to cover a big loop to the south and north of Prince George. I went south first, found nothing, then headed in the opposite direction with the intention of going as far as Fort Ware north of the Williston Reservoir. I was northeast of the main industrial section of Prince George when I spotted something that didn't fit. There was smoke coming from a pulp mill and two sawmills but I had spotted something else.

As I approached I could see the flames from a farmer's burning slash pile starting to spread through a field towards the forest. In another 10 minutes it would be into the bush. Normally we wouldn't douse fires on private property but this blaze was soon going to involve Crown land. I picked up a load of water from the Fraser River, planning to come in fast at about 50 feet and spread the water over a long distance just ahead of the flames.

I climbed above the river embankment and that's when I saw the farmer. He'd arrived while I was loading and was trying to create a fire break with a small bulldozer along the same line where I needed to drop the water. I was coming up behind him so he couldn't see me and the noise from the bulldozer probably meant he couldn't hear me either. In a pilot's life there are lots of decisions that need to be made in just a fraction of a second. I came to put out a fire and that's what I had to do, dropping all 200 gallons from 50 feet, just behind the bulldozer. I circled after the drop and didn't see any fist waving or obvious cursing so maybe he had appreciated the cool shower and help with the fire. I did a wing wave and carried on north to Fort Ware.

By the time I approached Prince George on the return leg of the spotting mission, the evening sky was beginning to show. I was still about 40 miles from the city when I saw what looked like a bright orange diamond up ahead. At first I just thought I'd been flying too long and was starting to imagine things. But the diamond grew larger as I got closer. Eventually I was able to put it together. A huge log jam on the Fraser River was burning and I had been seeing its reflection in the water. The fire was burning so hot there was no smoke.

I found a good water pick-up area about three miles to the south on the river and dropped load after load on the burning log jam until I had it down to a smoulder. By the time I finished it was getting very close to dark. However, while bombing the log jam, I had noticed smoke rising from the trees on one bank of the river. So I dropped two more loads into the trees and killed that fire.

I usually called into the Forest Service with a report on my daily activities but it was now so late I couldn't raise anyone on the radio. I decided I'd notify them in the morning and complete my log books then. I arrived at work early the next day and was writing in my log when I got a call from the Forest Service office congratulating me on putting out the log jam fire. This surprised me because I hadn't told anyone about my activities on the previous day except Toni. So I asked the caller how he had found out so soon.

His answer was a good one. As we spoke on the phone there were three rather annoyed First Nations fishermen standing in front of him. They had been smoking a substantial amount of salmon, he told me, just in from the bank of the river near the log jam when the Otter came over twice, dousing their fire, ruining their fish and soaking them. "Unfortunate," I said, and I meant it. "But where there's smoke, there's fire and it's my job to put it out."

If there is such a thing as karma, then the boaters, the farmer and the fishermen have been avenged. Shortly after the above mentioned incidents I was called to douse a fire burning on a steep, grassy slope. I decided to start at the top of the hill and, with more speed than usual, try to spread a long string of water down the slope just ahead of the fire. The excessive speed and the nose-down position of the plane was not a good idea. Instead of dropping onto the fire, the water came gushing back into the airplane soaking me and the whole cockpit area. I settled for a more conventional approach to the fire after that – a lateral attack with a drop speed of about 80 miles an hour.

Another time I was picking up water from the Fraser River between two sets of well separated rapids. I had picked up five loads and touched down for my sixth when I was hit with a blast of water that obliterated my view of the instrument panel and left me sloshing around in the cockpit. At first I thought I'd dumped the aircraft in the river so I closed down the throttle. That got me off the step and I slowed down to a taxi. That's when the water stopped hitting me and I could actually see what was happening. One of the two filler tubes that scooped water from the river and delivered it into the tank had dislodged and was pointing right at me. Soaked to the skin, I now had to spend a considerable amount of time removing both tubes before I could take off. It would have been an easy job on shore but I couldn't beach the aircraft anywhere on this stretch of river. So I had to keep the plane taxiing up the middle of the river while I stood outside on the floats removing the tubes. I was in and out of the cockpit several times, redirecting the plane to the centre of the river, before the job was done and I could fly home for repairs.

Those were the most memorable soakings endured while fire fighting but the job afforded many more opportunities for adventure. I was once called to a fire burning in a valley bottom which presented some real problems in terms of getting close to the flames. If I started my approach from the steep slope at the head of the valley I couldn't get low enough for an effective hit on the fire. Dropping water from too high an elevation meant it would just evaporate before getting to the flames.

*The start of a huge forest fire between Telegraph Creek and Dease Lake. It created so much smoke and ash that planes could not take off from Dease Lake for a day.*

Since the valley floor was not too steep I decided to fly up the valley instead of down, reasoning that once I'd dumped my water I would have enough power to climb out of the valley before reaching the steep section at the end.

It was an okay plan but it had a flaw. There was no alternate escape route if anything went wrong during the bombing run. And when do things go wrong? Right – when you don't have an escape plan. I took on my load, flew up the valley, pulled the lever to release the water and the handle broke. A big something had definitely gone wrong. I was in fate's hands. Fortunately the door on the tank had been partially released when I had pulled on the handle. It took a few seconds but water pressure on the partially opened door forced it the rest of the way and the tank emptied. The load totally missed the fire but at least I was alive and able to climb out of harm's way. I flew home for repairs to the release handle and vowed never again to embark on low-level flying without an escape plan.

I also had to drop my water and run while fighting a fire along a road near Fort Nelson. I was trying to keep the fire from crossing the road and running off through the trees to the south. It was early morning and the fire was down but there was lots of smoke along the advancing edge. I had dropped six loads and was coming in with a seventh, probably too low to the ground, when the smoke burst into a wall of flame. The heat dropped my left wing and the plane veered towards the burning trees. It was so hot I could feel the heat through the Plexiglas windshield. I also had to worry about the engine losing power, or quitting altogether, as it sucked in that hot, oxygen-depleted air. I did the only thing I could. I dumped the load and got an immediate lift. I could climb now so I turned to the right and scrambled out of there as quickly as possible. The fire wall had grown too big for the Otter to make any significant difference so I called for a ground crew to take over.

I can remember another time I had to retreat while fighting a fire but it was not the flames that chased me off. I was picking up water on Eagle Lake, west of Prince George. The lake was aptly named as I had spotted about a dozen occupied eagles' nests in the trees around the shoreline. After my third pass the eagles had had enough of my racket and started attacking the aircraft. I went in search of another lake. No pilot needs a bird the size of an eagle smashing through his windshield.

There was one occasion, however, when I almost had a duck take the co-pilot's seat. I was making a landing at the Prince George airport early in the spring and a few puddles had formed near the approach to the runway. A small flock of ducks rose up off one of the puddles just as I was coming in. I pulled up to over fly them, but one came through the prop, flew over the windshield, leaving his calling card on the glass, and then took out the radio antennas. I never went back to see if it had survived, but it must have had very good timing to go through the prop and not get clipped by one of the blades.

Turn around time was always an important consideration when water bombing fires. The whole point of using the Otter was its ability to get to a fire quickly, pick up water from spots the bigger planes couldn't use and hit the fire frequently over a short period of time. We usually did our pick ups from lakes and rivers but one time I opted for a new source.

The fire was running through the bush alongside a rancher's field west of Quesnel. The nearest lake was 15 miles away which would mean a turn around time of about 12 minutes. This was too long. However, spring run off had flooded the rancher's field to a depth of about three feet. I knew this because just the tops of the fence posts were showing. There was a swamp at the north end of field but it was too short for a safe pick up. So I took another look at the field and judged it long enough to pick up water, clear the fence at the end of the field and then use the swamp area to gain altitude.

It worked perfectly. My turn around time was three to four minutes. Within 40 minutes I had dropped 2,000 gallons on the fire and on the surrounding area to prevent a flare up.

Eventually the bigger Bell Jet Ranger helicopters took over our supply runs and bigger planes than the Otter, able to carry huge amounts of fire retardant, took over the water bombing runs. I actually think this was a mistake. I've saved a lot of timber by arriving at a fire quickly and hitting it in its infancy. The bigger bombers were usually stationed in the southern part of the province and it could take hours to get them up north. I also think we could have mixed fire retardant with our water to improve the efficiency of our drops. It works to both smother a fire and to impede its progress, even after the retardant has dried up on the ground. And it also serves as a fertilizer for new growth at the fire site.

After I left Prince George I did continue my work fighting forest fires but from the ground this time, not from the air. It was a kind of semi-retirement job and lasted for seven years after I quit flying commercially. Each year, from April to November, I worked for the BC Forest Service overseeing operations at the air tanker bases in Burns Lake, Smithers, Terrace and Dease Lake.

I travelled between these bases and was essentially responsible for ensuring the safe and efficient loading of the air tankers whenever they were fighting fires in the Northwest. This meant I handled training for the loading crews, made sure there were always adequate supplies of tools, equipment, fuel, water and fire retardant at the bases and checked the configuration of the pumps which had to deliver the exact ratios of water and retardant into the planes' holding tanks. This was a big job when you were servicing a DC-6, capable of hauling 2,500 gallons of retardant, or the Fire Cats which carried 725 gallons. The retardant came in by tanker truck from Kamloops and we could easily go through a whole truckload in a day.

Sometimes I had to draw on my engineering experience, to plan and oversee the construction of new water wells, fences, piping for spill ponds, and parking lots at the tanker bases. During one high fire season we even had to run pipelines from a small lake near the Dease Lake airport to the tanker base in order to supply enough water to fight the fires. This was challenging work and I enjoyed it very much. It brought me into close contact with aircraft again and called upon many of the skills I had learned over almost 40 years in the aviation industry.

I do remember one occasion, however, back when we were still using just water, when I had to check the skill level of a fellow pilot on water drops. No point in wasting the water, I thought, so we picked up a few loads and tried dropping them on a friend's potato patch near Chief Lake, a little northwest of Prince George. With water drops timing is everything; the slightest miscalculation means the water will miss the target. My pilot was pulling the release lever too soon and therefore missing my friend's garden with every pass. After a few of these unsuccessful drops I told my student to wait for my signal and then pull the lever. Just as I hollered, I stuck my head out of the window to see where the water fell. We did soak his spuds on that pass but the wind tore the aviator's sunglasses right off my face and carried them away.

A week later Toni and I went to visit my friend at Chief Lake. I went out to the garden in a vain attempt to find what I suspected would be my smashed sunglasses and found them, undamaged, lying on the leaves of one of the potato plants.

*Bill getting ready to take off with a load of skydivers.*

It was not only water and supplies we dropped from airplanes. For two years in a row I was booked to drop a group of six parachutists over the Prince George Fall Fair. Some days all six would plop right into the designated drop zone. And then there were those other days! One time, not one of the parachutists managed to land in the drop zone. One of the chaps landed on the hood of a car in the fairgrounds parking lot and another got hung up in a tree outside the fence. One broke his ankle, sidelining himself for the rest of the week. Then his replacement gave us all a scare. He had trouble with the rip cord and fell a long way before managing to deploy his chute and land without injury. At one point I was sure he was going straight into the trees.

For these parachute flights I was supposed to climb no higher than 4,500 feet to avoid conflict with other air traffic. But the group always wanted me to go higher so they could free fall before opening their chutes. Each day I would sneak a little above the limit but on the last day

I climbed to 9,000 feet. The control tower at the airport had me on the radio almost immediately asking for my elevation. I told them 4,500 feet. I could then hear them chuckling as they knew full well how high I was. They were watching the drop with binoculars from the airport.

People who jump out of airplanes for fun tend to be enthusiastic recruiters for their sport. These guys were always trying to get me to join them for a jump. I would decline, saying someone had to fly the plane even though there were three other pilots around at the time. I always told them only a crazy person would jump out of a perfectly good airplane.

# Takeoff Dolly

Every spring Pacific Western would have to fly its Prince George planes to Vancouver to have them converted from wheel skis to floats. Then, in the fall, we had to go south again to reverse the process.

These were bothersome and expensive trips, especially in the fall. First, weather was unpredictable between Prince George and Vancouver at that time of year. And, if we had to wait too long for good flying weather, ice would begin forming on the river and we'd be dodging ice floes on takeoff. Once we got to Vancouver, and the landing gear was

*The two midnight Beavers at the old Prince George airstrip alongside Highway 16.*

converted, weather could again delay our departure for home and the company would have to pay for us to stay until the weather cleared.

One fall I decided there was another way. We would do the conversion ourselves at our dock on the Fraser River by Fort George Park. The first part went quite well. We hired a small crane to lift two Beavers and replaced the floats with wheels. Now we had to get the planes to our base at the main airport east of town. No problem, I figured. We'll wait until after midnight and then taxi them along the mostly deserted streets from the river to the old airfield beside Highway 16, just west of its intersection with Highway 97. In the morning we would fly them to the main airport.

This plan also worked well, with a bit of problem solving. At one

*Ice and snow at the float plane dock in Prince George. CF-FHB (left), the original de Havilland Beaver, with its PWA paint job.*

intersection we had trouble with the spacing between a couple of telephone poles but worked it out by swinging one wing through the poles, then turning the tail backwards and swinging the other wing through. Not unexpectedly, a few lights came on inside houses and a few heads poked out of doors. Two 450 horsepower Pratt & Whitney engines rumbling through your neighbourhood at 2 a.m. are bound to cause a stir. At one place, where the occupant came outside, one of our engineers shouted, "Which way to Vancouver?" We thought for sure that guy would call the police but they never showed up. Probably we should have notified them but it never occurred to us, nor did the idea of bringing along a camera to record this historic journey.

Our next challenge was figuring how to get the planes back onto the river in the spring without first flying to Vancouver. We could easily convert from wheel-skis to floats at our Prince George base but we needed a way to take off from the runway on floats. This is when I came up with the idea of a takeoff dolly.

Flying is at low ebb in winter so I had lots of time to design the thing.

*A Beaver on the takeoff dolly at Prince George airport.*

First I laid out a pattern on the hangar floor for the tubular frame and then chose a set of Beaver wheels for the main gear and two, small tail-wheel assemblies for the front gear. The bigger wheels would support the weight of the plane and the front wheels would be used to steer. With the help of engineers and a professional welder we put those parts together.

I then designed two big wooden blocks with a deep V cut into them and lined the Vs with carpet. This is where the floats would sit, their metal bottoms cushioned by the carpet. Once the blocks were mounted on the dolly and the whole thing assembled, we tested it by pushing it down the runway with a pick-up truck. I used bungee cords to stabilize the front wheels and keep the dolly moving in a straight line. If it veered to right or left after takeoff, Murphy's Law dictated it would smash into one of the runway lights.

The braking system consisted of one of those eight-foot diameter parachutes we used for air drops to firefighters. I tied the chute to the back of the dolly frame in the middle with a 10-foot length of rope. A string attached the chute to the airplane. When the plane lifted off the dolly, the string would pull the ripcord deploying the chute and the chute would slow the dolly as it sped down the runway under the plane. I was going to put a hydraulic brake on the dolly but the chute system worked

*Bill poses for the camera before testing the takeoff dolly for the first time.*

well and, besides, it reminded me of the braking system the US Air Force used on their fighter jets – sexy and dramatic.

The day finally arrived when it was time to get the Beavers down to the river. The head office in Vancouver, to put it kindly, was less than supportive of my initiative, suggesting my future with the company would be uncertain if anything went wrong. And, of course, someone had tipped off the press concerning the dolly's first real test. Even the CBC was there with its television cameras. I did a few slow taxi tests, just to get the feel of riding so much higher, and then took off. The lift off went perfectly and as I reached the end of the runway I banked hard so I could see where the dolly went. That's when one of the CBC cameras filmed me and the clip made it onto the evening news.

The next day I got a phone call from a friend with the Department of Transport asking, in jest, why I'd been doing aerobatics at the end of the runway without first obtaining the proper permit.

Word of the dolly's success found its way to Vancouver. Instead of the rogue pilot risking company aircraft, I was now the golden boy and would I please send the plans for my great new invention to head office. I did and the plans were forwarded to company bases in Edmonton and Terrace. A year later I was in Edmonton and taken to see what was now billed as the Vancouver engineering department's brilliant, new takeoff dolly. Even my plans had been signed by PWA's chief engineer. I soon set the Edmonton crew straight on who had designed, built, tested and baptised the dolly and I had pictures to prove it. But the whole episode left a bad taste in my mouth, especially when I knew the dolly was saving the company a lot of money.

Eventually, after using the dolly several times, I trusted it enough to take off with a full load of freight. Loading at our main base rather than down on the river made things much easier, but I never used the dolly if I was carrying passengers.

I already mentioned the longer prop and the bigger skis I helped get for our planes but there were other things I developed that either simplified winter operations in the north or made them more comfortable. For instance, I bought a war surplus cabin heater, which had been used to keep soldiers warm in the back of troop trucks, and adapted it for use as an engine heater. The cabin heater ran on gasoline and had an automatic fuel start and ignition. I hung a quart of gasoline, with a line to the heater, from a wing strut, set the heater up about 10 feet back from the plane and piped hot air from the heater to the space under the engine tent with a 10 foot length of five-inch ducting. When the temperature dropped to minus 20 C or below I was able to warm up the plane's engine in about

20 minutes. Before this, we used open-flame blow pots set up under the engine. The engine had to be covered with a section of canvas and the pilot had to climb under this makeshift tent and stay there to ensure the flaming blow-pots didn't set the canvas or anything else on fire. It was horrible under there, breathing in all the fumes from the blow pots.

Another winter problem was air leakage from the wheel-ski cylinders on the Beavers and Otters. The solution to this one was simple. I bought a high-pressure air strut pump by mail order from Princess Auto. The cylinders were initially filled with nitrogen but in the bush we had no hesitation about using air if it was going to make the difference between getting home or not.

My last rig up was a little invention to warm up the cabin area of the Beaver when flying in really cold weather. The plane had its own heating system that operated on ram air from the plane's forward motion. But all of the curves in the inlet pipe, which entered the cabin area via a duct in the floor, meant not much warm air made it into the plane. On a cold day it was below freezing in the cabin. So I took the blower from a big car heater and mounted it over the heat duct in the cabin area. This brought in more warm air which I could then direct onto the windshield or down to warm my feet. And the cabin was cosy.

There was just one little glitch. The blower was not an approved installation so we had to remove it after each flight. And, of course, I forgot to remove it one day and that was the day the Department of Transport inspector examined our planes. Within days I got a call from the Vancouver office advising me never to use the blower again.

# "I" Sites on the DEW Line

One summer I had the good fortune to fly a Beaver out of Cape Parry on Canada's Distant Early Warning (DEW) Line, about 600 miles north of Yellowknife. Designed to protect Canada and the United States from enemy air attack from the north, the DEW Line consisted of 63 radar and communication sites spaced 50 miles apart and stretching for 3,000 miles from the northwest coast of Alaska to the eastern shore of Baffin Island, roughly along the 69th parallel.

*The Cape Parry airstrip.*

Summer is late in the Arctic. Since I was on floats I had to delay my arrival until the beginning of July when the ice melted off a little lake adjacent to the community's main runway. Referred to as a main station, Cape Parry was actually a small town plopped in the middle of nowhere. Two hundred men (and no women) lived there, housed in long barracks called trains that were elevated on stilts to prevent melting of the permafrost. Within the train each man had his own room. These were modern, well-equipped structures with sofas, pianos, and pool tables for comfort and entertainment.

*Inside one of the trains.*

When I was there the employees used a little, flat-topped island of rock just off shore from the community as a heavy equipment storage facility. Since it was connected to the mainland by a narrow neck of land, it wasn't really an island. You could actually drive to it safely if there wasn't a fierce storm blowing. One time, when one of those hurricane-force storms grounded me for three days in a row, I suggested to the Cape's RCMP officer that the island of rock would be a good place to get pictures of the storm. We were a bit bored after three days of inactivity. Within minutes we were into his Land Rover and on our way.

I was right about the island as a good vantage point for storm pictures. I have shots of water flying 50 feet over our heads as waves smashed into the rocks 70 feet below us. And I almost had a picture of the RCMP officer losing his Land Rover. He had neglected to engage the emergency brake. With our attention focussed elsewhere, we didn't notice when the wind started the vehicle rolling towards the cliff-edge. There was a bit of a scramble, disaster was averted and we were no longer bored. On our way back we waited for about 10 waves to crash over the neck of land before we could sneak through to safety.

*Rock promontory at Cape Parry during a storm.*

Personnel, mail, food, and equipment were transported in a DC-3 or DC-4 from Edmonton to Cape Parry. My job was to shuttle whatever needed delivering, especially the mail, to six intermediate, or "I" sites, three on either side of the main station. I landed either in bays along the shoreline of the Arctic Ocean or on small lakes near the "I" sites when I made deliveries. In some ways flying the DEW Line reminded me of flying the west coast of Vancouver Island when I was stationed at Port Alberni. It could be a hot summer afternoon and all of a sudden dense fog would roll in off the Arctic Ocean accompanied by 30 to 50 mile an hour winds. I always kept a parka in the plane as the temperature could drop as much as 15 degrees C when one of these fog banks came in. On more than one occasion I had to detour to a small lake about 20 miles south of Cape Parry and wait for the fog to lift off the coastline. It would usually take about an hour and then the fog would rise 100 feet and I could fly home under it. Light was never a problem. The sun wouldn't set at all until the beginning of August and we wouldn't get full nights until September. Twenty-four hour days could be disorienting if you weren't paying attention. On one occasion I'd been working for hours and hours and lost all track of time. I showed up for lunch at midnight and couldn't understand why no one else was there.

Visibility could also be deceiving in the Arctic. There were times when I would radio one of the radar "I" sites to report I was about five miles out only to be told I was 20 miles out on their screen. Since the Beaver didn't have radar, and I'd never heard of a GPS (global positioning system) back then, I depended on charts and visual landmarks for navigation. I can remember taking off from the water and seeing light from a communications tower 50 miles away. I think this was due to clear air and the flatness of the terrain. On one flight I could see Banks Island as if it were a stone's throw from the mainland while, in fact, it was 70 miles from the Cape Parry station. If there had been caribou on the shore of the island, I'm sure I would have seen them.

Of course, visibility could also be very bad. I once had to transport a doctor from Cape Parry 250 miles southwest to Inuvik to help out in the aftermath of a helicopter crash. We took off about two a.m. into low overcast and rain. Visibility was only two or three miles with a bit of patchy ground fog. Adding to the difficulty was the fact I'd never flown this route before. We flew about 200 to 300 feet above the ground which meant the "I" site radar operators, who were anxious about our position, couldn't pick us up on their screens. I would then climb to 500 feet, where they could pick me up on both the radar and the radio. However, at 500 feet, I had no visibility due to cloud and had to descend. It was a roller-coaster ride but we made it to Inuvik about two hours after takeoff.

Weather was not an issue as I returned to Cape Parry later that day but another problem was evident. Uncountable, migrating snow geese, so many they posed a real hazard to aviation, filled the sky. I had never seen so many birds in one area and it wasn't until I climbed to 5,000 feet that I got above them and out of harm's way. I took a picture of the geese from above as they crossed a lake and am still momentarily confused every time I look at the picture now; the lake looks to be covered in thousands upon thousands of whitecaps.

I often saw wildlife while flying in the Arctic. The Mackenzie Delta is covered with thousands of little lakes. During breeding season, when you see a lone Canada goose on one of those lakes, you know it's a gander and there's a nesting female in the grass somewhere nearby. I have seen a herd of 20 muskoxen circling to protect their young and wolves and foxes hunting in the nesting grounds of swans and geese. And there was a great abundance of good-sized fish in the small lakes in the Cape Parry area. I have pictures of the camp boss holding a fish at waist height and the tail is touching the ground.

In fact, it was an aborted fishing trip that led to my discovery of a problem with the Beaver that had been nagging me for some time. One weekend a group of camp employees wanted to go fishing. I didn't feel up to the trip so a pilot from Edmonton volunteered to take them. He was half-way through the takeoff when he realized he wouldn't get off the water and decided to abort. He ended up in the rocks on the far side of the float plane lake.

I had been experiencing slow takeoffs for some time and had been checking the engine for problems. I had to pump water out of the floats every day but didn't really think this was causing the plane's sluggishness. However, after that pilot went onto the rocks, I had to give the floats a really thorough inspection. That's when I discovered the drain tubes in four of the compartments had cracks in them. This meant I could never pump out all of the water; ten gallons or more would remain in each of the four damaged compartments amounting to between 400 and 500 pounds of extra weight.

The cracks weren't the Edmonton pilot's fault. They occur when the floats are removed in the fall and stored outside. Rainwater seeps in, freezes and cracks the tubes. No one thought to remove the compartment covers in the spring and check for damage.

*Inuit children at Cape Parry.*

If summer comes late to the Arctic, fall comes early. By mid-September ice on the float plane lake forced me to move the Beaver into a bay on Cape Parry's ocean front. I waited out stormy weather for a week and then took off in rough seas with about 500 pounds of ice clinging to the sides of the plane and the floats. I couldn't chip it off without hurting the plane and knew it would wear off in flight anyway. I was headed home after being away from my family for three months. I stopped to fuel up at Great Bear Lake and then flew on to Yellowknife, the hub of the north, where, in September of 1959, I'd filled in for two weeks for a fellow pilot who went on vacation.

*The float plane dock at Yellowknife, NWT.*

That had been my first experience flying the Arctic – the land was flat, radio beacons were few and far between, and careful map reading was essential. The local pilots advised me to draw a line on a map and stick to it, using only the bigger lakes as check points.

My first trip was to Contwoyto Lake, about 250 miles north of Yellowknife, on a charter for Indian Affairs. It took us about two hours to get there and when we did the Indian agent told me to fly the shoreline. This was odd. I figured he would know the location of the village but I did what he said and before long we saw a group of Inuit on the shore. This is when I learned that an Inuit's parka, at least at this time of year, was his home and that these people were constantly on the move.

We landed on the lake but I couldn't taxi to shore due to shallow water and large boulders. I shut down and soon two men waded out and carried the Indian agent ashore. I stayed with the plane. After about an hour, and a cup of tea for the agent, two men returned to the plane – the agent and an elderly man who needed dental work in the city.

The man was 65-year-old Joe Otoyuk and I figured this was his first trip to Yellowknife. He was fascinated by the roads and power lines as we neared the city. When we drove into town from our float base on Great Slave Lake he asked the driver to stop at the sight of some children playing on bicycles. The Indian agent had a hard time explaining the principles of bike riding to Joe and why they would not work in the barren lands. I found out later he was very disappointed in not being able to buy some bikes for his grandchildren.

At supper that night we suggested Joe might like the salmon. He had no trouble with the fish but before we could stop him he ate the lemon slices, rind and all. I don't think he was too comfortable with the knives and forks either, preferring an ulu, or curved knife, and his fingers. But he adapted quickly. The next day at the hotel he was dressed in a wool shirt, denim pants and logger's boots. I didn't recognize him until he called my name and spoke to me. And he quickly picked up the city way of dining. A week later, using money he had earned hunting wolves, Joe chartered an Otter, filled it with a load of plywood and other building materials and headed home. I never saw the shelters he built but I expect they were unique in his neighbourhood.

It seemed every time I turned around on that posting to Yellowknife I learned something new. For instance, I couldn't understand why I was being given lucrative, long-distance trips to Norman Wells, about 425 miles west of Yellowknife, when I was lowest on the local seniority chart. After the first trip I just figured the pilots were a generous bunch who liked to share. Then it happened again, this time while two of the local guys were waiting for flights. When I asked, the pilots told me they hated flying over the mountains between Yellowknife and Norman Wells. To me, these were just rolling hills. Flying at 4,000 feet would clear them all.

I also got to fly a Beaver on floats to Coppermine, about 380 miles northwest of Yellowknife on the Coronation Gulf. It was the mail run and took about four hours each way. As the water was too shallow to beach the plane, a couple of Inuit men came out in a boat to unload mail and freight. They also carried a fuel drum so I could refuel the plane.

My time flying the Arctic was short but memorable. I had read about Arctic bush pilots for years and appreciated deeply the opportunity to live their lifestyle, even for a short while, and to meet some of the people who thrive in what many of us would consider a very inhospitable, yet undeniably beautiful environment. As a post-script to that assignment in Yellowknife I should mention that my route back to Prince George took me over Wood Buffalo National Park. It was the first time I had ever seen bison and I was mightily impressed by these huge animals with their wool-ringed necks and massive horns.

# For Better or for Worse

I worked for Pacific Western Airlines out of Prince George from 1957 through 1967 when they closed down all of the visual flight rules (VFR) bases in the west. In that year we moved to Telkwa in the Bulkley Valley, about 240 miles west of Prince George, and I started flying for Bill Harrison's Omineca Airlines on Tyhee Lake, just east of my new home town. We had two Otters, two Beavers and a Cessna 185 at the Tyhee base and used them for fire fighting, fishing and hunting charters, geological exploration and to transport government officials to various sites in the North. Bill eventually sold Omineca to Trans-Provincial Airlines in Terrace and I worked for them until 1974 when I started flying occasionally for Smithers Air Services Ltd. That company was owned by Emil Mesich and also based at Tyhee Lake. It was after I quit flying for Emil that I took the tanker base job with the BC Forest Service.

In reviewing my log books for all of those years I realize there were some incidents, and some people, worth remembering. And, as with any job, some I'd like to forget. Most of the incidents I'd like to forget are the ones which required me to complete reports filled with excruciating detail about how things went miserably, and expensively, wrong. But before I get into the aviation mishaps, I should mention our move to Telkwa.

I moved first and Toni followed once the kids had finished school for the year. All went well until it came time to move our three horses from Prince George to a ranch not too far from Telkwa. Toni hired a

*Bill in the 1970s.*

cowboy friend with a big truck who figured it would take about five hours to complete the move. Just east of Vanderhoof the engine blew up. No problem. They called our friend Leonard Ongman who drove out from Prince George, taxied them into Vanderhoof and then waited while they hired another truck. Then they drove back to the first truck, transferred the horses and set off once again, leaving the broken truck at the side of the road. As evening set in they realized there was a problem with the headlights on the new truck so they pulled to the side of the road again, forced to wait for the first light of morning. Toni was now hand feeding the horses and hauling water for them.

They arrived at the Tyhee float plane base about 8:30 on a Saturday morning, sleep deprived and a tad crusty, just as I was taxiing out into the lake for takeoff. Toni walked into the office and asked where I was. When they told her I was about to take off she told them with some force to get me back and damned fast. Fortunately, fellow pilot Grant Luck agreed to do the flight which freed me up to guide Toni, the cowboy and the horses to the ranch. And, after we paid for a long list of towing charges, wages, parts and repairs, including an engine rebuild on the first truck, our move to Telkwa was complete.

That little "five-hour" trip cost us a fortune but, unlike the time I was flying some Forest Service personnel to Hudson's Hope, I didn't have to complete a stack of accident reports. Pacific Western flew to Hudson's Hope daily during the Williston project with a Twin Beechcraft on wheels and also did charters with the Beavers and Otters on floats. On the day in question I was getting ready to land an Otter on the Peace River when we encountered an isolated summer storm that forced me to land above the cable ferry crossing. That meant I had to taxi downriver and under the cable in order to get to the Hudson's Hope float plane dock. Just as I was about to go under the cable, the ferry started to cross, pulled the cable down and tore off part of the Otter's rudder, dumping it into the river. No one was hurt and I taxied to the dock but it took three days to obtain and install a replacement part. And then came the accident reports for the Vancouver office.

More paperwork was required after an aborted flight from Prince George to Fort Nelson in marginal weather, again with a plane load of Forest Service personnel. I was flying a twin-engine Widgeon just under the clouds when the weather turned really sour around Trutch, about 80 miles south of Fort Nelson. I opted to turn back and wait it out at Fort St.

John and that's when my right engine started banging and sputtering. It didn't completely quit but I was getting little power out of it. I was about 400 feet above the road and had just passed an abandoned airstrip. The centre of the strip looked good so I decided to land but a wicked cross wind forced me to correct to the right, into my nearly dead engine. As I lowered the wheels and flaps, the cross wind kept pushing me left. I had the right wing down to correct for the drift. In fact it was down so far, the float at the tip of the wing was hitting the runway and still I could not correct for the left drift. That's when some boulders hidden in the brush on the left side of the runway tore off my left landing gear. We cruised to a stop on the plane's keel minus half our landing gear, with a damaged right wing and only one engine. I found out later a nut and some pieces of metal had come loose in the right engine's air intake manifold. They were sucked into the engine and damaged the piston and valves in two cylinders. As I said, more paperwork.

I'm not a particularly superstitious man but I did have cause to wonder one day when a fellow at Babine Lake put a curse on me. It was the winter of 1973 and I was doing the mail run for Trans-Provincial out of Telkwa to Fort Babine and Takla Landing. That run was usually done using the Cessna 180 but it was already busy so I took an Otter. I landed at Fort Babine and encountered a fellow who wanted a lift over to Takla. He was almost too drunk to stand so I refused. There was no way I was going to have someone that inebriated aboard without a third and sober person to keep things under control. My refusal did not go over well, some words were exchanged and as I turned to leave he said, "I hope you crash."

I carried on to Takla, delivered the mail, had coffee with the manager of the trading post and picked up an order for the Goodacre's grocery store in Smithers before heading home. Jim Goodacre delivered the order to our base early that afternoon so I loaded up about a ton of groceries and flew back to Takla, all without incident.

However, things fell apart, literally, when I tried to take off from the lake. Just as I reached lift-off speed, the right undercarriage collapsed. This dropped my right wing onto the snow but, more importantly, the propeller dropped too, cutting through the snow and into the ice before I could shut down the engine. It was bent beyond repair. I radioed our dispatcher and hitched a ride back to base with pilot Scot Cameron who was flying over Bear Lake en route to Smithers. Three days later we repaired the damage with parts flown in to Takla from Trans-Provincial's Terrace base and then flew the Otter back to Terrace for a thorough inspection.

In one way, the curse had worked. But it could have been a lot worse. What if I'd actually lifted off the lake? The dangling ski could have done a lot more damage to the plane and I would have had to try landing on one ski.

Lady Luck, and a good understanding of engine mechanics, saved the day again on a flight out of a lake about 80 miles east of Prince George. The lake is situated in a deep valley and is drained by a creek at one end. I was flying an Otter on floats with eight passengers on board and had just turned down the creek when I noticed the windshield was turning black. I had an oil leak. The gauge was fluctuating. I was in mountainous terrain with no obvious place to land and I really wanted to be home for supper that night.

*The cursed and then crippled Otter at Takla Landing.*

I looked out the side window and saw that the wing was also black. That meant the oil was spewing out through a broken propeller seal. I immediately pulled the propeller lever into coarse pitch which effectively shuts off oil to the prop and activates a set of counter weights. This stabilized the gauge – a good sign – but I now had much less climbing power. The engine is set at about 2,300 revolutions per minute (rpms) for takeoff and you need about 2,000 rpms to climb. But in coarse pitch you only have about 1,500 rpms. That's cruising power but not enough to climb to a safe height above the trees or return to the lake.

That's when luck took over. I hit a few updrafts, which got us clear of the tree tops, and then the terrain was all downhill to the Fraser River. I was actually able to nurse the plane all the way home. The Otter holds nine gallons of oil. I figure we had lost about half of it in the minute before I cut off the supply to the prop. Another minute and I would have been missing more than my supper.

Repairing airplanes in the bush is difficult work. Trying to avoid it keeps one alert to the unexpected. One time I was trying to take off from Cunningham Lake, about 30 miles north of Burns Lake. I had just dropped off a couple of geologists and had two more to drop at a little lake about 10 miles to the west. Storm force winds were churning up huge waves so I opted to use the protection of a small island for takeoff. I opened the throttle and pulled back on the stick to raise the nose and put the aircraft into planing mode. I had travelled only 100 feet when a big gust of wind lifted the plane about 75 feet off the surface of the water. I was now in a stall condition; the right wing dropped and we hit the water hard on the right float, snapping all the struts on that side of the plane. With no support, the right wing should have fallen into the water but I'd pushed hard on the right rudder on impact. The shore of the island was about seven feet high and only a few yards away. Just as we reached it, the wing collapsed onto a pinnacle of rock which punched a hole in the aluminum and held us to the shore. This gave me a chance to jump out and tie the plane to a big tree stump.

I radioed the air base at Telkwa and an Otter was dispatched to rescue us. It was still much too rough for that plane to get close so the pilot put down across the lake at a fishing camp and enlisted the help of a guide to pick us up by boat. When the wind died down we flew the remaining two geologists to their drop off point.

Now I had to rescue the plane. Company engineers and I brought in new struts and skin for the wing. Since the pinnacle of rock held the wing up, replacing the struts wasn't too difficult. We just filled the right float with enough water to partially submerge it. This stretched things out enough to replace the struts without the aid of jacks and gin poles. Once the struts were in place we pumped the water out of the float, the plane rose and the wing lifted off the rock. We put a temporary patch over the hole in the wing and, three days after my hard landing, flew to Terrace for proper repairs.

It is not always weather and/or mechanical problems that age a pilot. Sometimes it's the customers. During the summer of 1959 there were forest fires burning everywhere around Prince George. Forest Service bureaucrats in Victoria were becoming increasingly concerned with the costs incurred to fight these blazes and sent a bean counter, who I'll call Mr. Gruff, to do something about all the expense. The Prince George office, believing the value of the threatened timber to be much higher

*Checking charts before takeoff.*

than the costs associated with saving it, decided Mr. Gruff needed to see first hand from the air what was at risk if he started cutting the budget. I was appointed as the pilot.

We took off for a big fire on the Parsnip River. I chose to fly a valley that hadn't been checked for a few days in case lightning strikes had started anything new. Under ordinary circumstances we would take a direct route to our destination. However, when trying to find fires, I would fly a zigzag route. This enabled spotters to see the area we had passed over as well as the ground ahead of us. The zigzag pattern also took advantage of differences in lighting as the plane changed direction, sometimes making it easier to see a small column of smoke. In all, this less direct line added about five minutes to our flight time to the Parsnip fire camp.

Mr. Gruff was not impressed, suggesting I was trying to build up my own air time with the company while maximizing revenue for Pacific Western.

After landing he, and a handful of other Forest Service personnel accompanying him, were taken on a tour of the Parsnip fire site. All were grim-faced when they returned to the plane an hour later. Mr. Gruff had not been convinced of the merits of the fire-fighting effort and the other Forest Service types were afraid his verdict on expenses would cost dearly in the loss of high-quality timber.

We took off upstream on the river and I chose another valley for our return trip to Prince George. No point in covering old ground, I thought, if we could create an opportunity to detect fires in another area. At about 500 feet I spotted a haze of smoke about 20 miles southeast of our route home. I reduced to cruise power, stayed at 500 feet, and headed for the smoke. Mr. Gruff, however, pulled out his maps and soon determined I was no longer taking the most direct and quickest route home. The silence from him and the other four in the back of the plane was deafening.

It took me about eight minutes to fly the 20 miles. I said nothing and kept the plane oriented so only I could see the smoke. As I got close I could see a column of smoke rising from the side of a river. In those days, my eyes were good enough to see a man lighting a cigarette from a mile away. As we got even closer I could see a second and then a third column of smoke, all caused by separate lightning strikes.

I banked the aircraft so all in the back could now see the three fires. There was immediate action. Maps came out of brief cases, hand held radios were flicked on and the exact location of the three strikes relayed to the Prince George fire control office. This did nothing to improve Mr. Gruff's mood. He put his maps away, crossed his arms over his chest and stared straight ahead with a disgusted look on his face. And it probably didn't help his disposition to realize his companions were elated with our timely discovery and reporting of the new fires. Even before we landed in Prince George a Beaver, carrying an initial attack crew, was on its way to the new fire area.

Mr. Gruff went home to Victoria that evening and, as far as I know, the Prince George fire fighting crews continued to hunt up new fires and hit them quickly. Sometimes, when a forest fire gets out of control, smoke will rise 25,000 to 30,000 feet. I have flown by fires whose winds have carried burning branches the size of your wrist, and six to eight feet long, as high as 12,000 feet. On one trip from Dease Lake to Prince George I could not see the ground from 10,000 feet because of the smoke. The only way I could navigate was from one column of smoke to another because I knew their locations relative to the ground.

There is definitely something to be said for spending the money up front when it comes to fighting forest fires. And it's not just the value of the timber. I often wondered how many animals were lost in fires that got hopelessly out of control and burned over hundreds of square miles.

In reality, we were trying to do Mr. Gruff a favour and he obviously didn't appreciate it. But that's not always the way. Sometimes a client's gratitude stays with you for ever.

It was a cool Saturday in December when I went down to the Tyhee Lake base. I had no particular task in mind but for some reason felt compelled to stop in. No one else was there but the radio was crackling and then I heard a voice I recognized. It was Anne Marie Nehring, a painter well-known in the Bulkley Valley, and she was calling for someone to please help her. She was up at Cold Fish Lake; something had happened to her eyes and she needed medical help right away.

I called Toni to let her know where I was going, filed a flight plan and was in the air 30 minutes after getting Anne Marie's call. It took me about an hour and 45 minutes to reach the lake and we were back at the base about four hours after the call.

A few months later Anne Marie asked how she could repay me. I said a portrait of my daughter Lynn would more than cover it and gave her a photo to paint from. Anne Marie also wanted to meet Lynn, to know her smile and personality, so I took her with me on a subsequent trip into Coldfish. Toni and I now have one of Anne Marie's finest portraits.

Pilots tend to be very careful in their work habits for obvious reasons. But sometimes your best efforts are sabotaged by fate. That's when you need special help and it came my way on a trip to Telegraph Creek. It was minus 35 C in the dead of winter, when the days are short and the weather unpredictable, and my heater had quit part way through the journey. I had flown a group of school children home for the Christmas holidays and landed on skis at the Telegraph Creek airstrip. We were all cold and the kids had scurried into warm cars and disappeared into the village as soon as we landed. I, on the other hand, was looking at another two hours in a freezing plane before I could get home. I tried to start the engine and nothing happened. The batteries were dead which meant the generator had quit. If I didn't get the engine started soon the cold would congeal the engine oil, I'd have to heat it up somehow and by then there would be no daylight left for the flight home. And there was no one left at the airstrip.

I was just about to walk for help when my guardian angel arrived. I don't remember now why he had come to the airstrip but he was driving a Land Rover and he had battery cables. He pulled up close enough to the plane that we could connect the cables and we got the plane started. It was an uncomfortable trip home, complicated by my having to turn off all electrical equipment, including instrument lights and radio, to conserve what little juice was left in the battery. It was dusk as I approached Terrace, too dark to see any of my unlit gauges, but I managed to get down using just my eyes to judge altitude and ground speed. It wasn't fun but much better than, say, weather forcing me down on some wilderness lake south of Telegraph with no way to call for help.

My career with Trans-Provincial ended in 1974. I had been flying an Otter off Tyhee Lake all through the summer of 1973 and, as we always did just before freeze up, flew the plane to Trans-Provincial's Terrace float base where it would be fitted out with wheel-skis for winter and kept at the Terrace airport. In January of '74 I was sent north to Mayo in the Yukon. I was to use the airport there as a base for hauling freight to some remote lakes in the northern part of the territory. I gathered up all my winter gear, headed for Terrace and picked up the Otter I'd flown all summer. Right away I noticed the plane was not running as well as when I'd flown it from Tyhee Lake to Terrace in the fall. I just figured it was the cold weather and carried on north to Mayo.

On my third trip north from Mayo the engine started to run more roughly. Since I was close to my destination I continued on to the target lake and landed. I unloaded the plane with the help of an assistant and then tried twice to take off for the flight back to Mayo. The engine would not produce enough power to accelerate to takeoff speed. I tried to radio the base in Mayo but got no answer so I tried taking off again and this time got the plane into the air.

We nursed it to as high an altitude as we could but still didn't get high enough to connect with the radio at Mayo. It took about two hours in the air, flying from lake to lake for safety, but we did manage to get back to the base.

I eventually found out what had happened. Not only had the engineers at Trans-Provincial's base in Terrace not winterized the plane, they had removed the nice clean spark plugs from my Otter and replaced them with very old and worn out ones from a plane based in Terrace. They had also switched props on me, giving me a shorter one that only had a few hours of serviceable time left on it. It should have been sent out for overhaul, not sent into the frozen north. A close inspection of the prop revealed there was a broken pin on one of the three blades. This meant the pitch angle on the damaged blade was finer than on the other two, again contributing to a rough running engine.

This could have resulted in a serious accident in harsh terrain with questionable access to help, all to save a few bucks. I quit the company after that incident.

And finally, in the "incidents worth remembering" category, here's another story about ducks. I was working on my home-built down at the Tyhee float plane base when seven ducks appeared between the floats. At one point I had to go back to my house for some parts and tools so I picked up some grain for the ducks. They gobbled it up and swam away when it was all gone. Two days later I came back to the dock to continue work on the plane. There were two pickup trucks beside the lake, a group of men talking on the shore and a flock of ducks about 100 yards out in the lake. As soon as my truck came into sight the ducks headed straight for the dock looking for more wheat. It was as if they actually recognized my vehicle. Of course, I had neglected to bring any grain and felt like a first class jerk.

# Ben Corke

No one could ever say working as a commercial pilot was a soft touch. We worked hard, often in miserable conditions, and we could be away from our families for months at a time. I remember being sent to Fort McMurray once to help fight a blaze in the tar sands. We were out of bed at four a.m. and the last flights were around midnight. If we weren't actually flying we were loading and unloading the aircraft and had little time to eat. I logged 180 hours over three weeks and by the time I got back to Prince George I was exhausted.

But we knew how to play too. One of my favourite diversions from work was the Pacific Logana Society, a group of about 25 people – Forest Service employees and pilots – who liked to spend time fishing in the mountains about 55 miles northeast of Prince George.

We preferred to fish Pacific Lake, one of three linked lakes all nestled between two mountains and straddling the divide between the Arctic and Pacific watersheds. We could canoe from Pacific Lake through a much smaller lake and into Arctic Lake. We never could understand why the Arctic grayling never migrated into the Pacific end of the chain – but they didn't.

We would load the Otter in Prince George with a group of anglers and a jug or two of Logana wine and land on Pacific Lake 30 minutes later. The designated pilot, of course, would stick to tea and/or coffee for the weekend. For accommodation we bought an old Pan Abode log building – once used as a PWA office in Hudson's Hope – flew it in pieces to the lake and put it up on the east shore alongside a creek. We built a small dam on the creek and used a hose to run fresh water from the newly-created reservoir to our kitchen. It was a comfortable place, capable of sleeping six to eight people, and the fishing was good. It was a perfect place to be after a summer of fighting forest fires. This whole area is now Arctic Pacific Lakes Provincial Park.

Another favourite social event was the annual "Thank you" party hosted by Pacific Western for the BC Forest Service. We fed more than 100 people every year serving local beef and cobs of sweet corn flown in from Kamloops. One year I was put in charge of making the coffee. Not too difficult, I thought. Just boil the water, toss in lots of coffee and let it brew a while. However, when it came time to throw in the coffee, I realized I'd purchased beans, not ground coffee, and there was no place open where I could grind them. I rushed home and picked up what coffee we had there and then proceeded to the homes of several other pilots, scrounging up whatever bits and drabs I could find. I think I had coffee from every coffee-producing nation in the world. It was definitely a strange brew but after all the alcohol consumed earlier that night, I doubt anyone noticed.

I also met many memorable and likeable people in my years flying the northern bush. One of them was Steele Hyland, who ran the store in Telegraph Creek and a lodge at the south end of Kinaskan Lake. Then there were guides like Einar Madsen on Babine Lake, Ray Collingwood and Bob Henderson, who were also pilots, Ron Flemming, and Bill Love of the Love Brothers and Lee outfit. The latter three all guided in the Tatlatui area and were a pleasure to work for. I will always remember the warm hospitality extended to me by Bill and Lil Love and Marty and Dorothy (Bill's sister) Allen and their families in the Kispiox Valley. Every year, when the guiding up north was finished, Bill would take me to his favourite steelhead hole in the Kispiox and I'd catch a couple of fish for mid-winter eating. Nor will I forget Herman Peterson from Atlin, a gifted craftsman who built his own airplane and also made violins that were cherished by the fiddlers of the North.

I also had the good fortune to fly my brother Richard as a PWA client. He lived in Prince George for a while and was responsible for monitoring summer flows and winter ice conditions on several rivers and streams in the area for Water Survey Canada, a branch of Environment Canada. In addition to being Richard's pilot I also helped him with his work, wrestling with a gas-power ice augur in the winter and stringing steel anchor cables across rivers in the summer. We would secure a cable to trees on either side of the river and then secure the boat to the cable while Richard took measurements of water temperature, flow rate and turbidity. When he was finished we'd move the cable to a new spot on the river and repeat the process.

Perhaps one of the most eccentric and complex characters I ever got to know was Ben Corke who, in 1956, bought the old Hudson's Bay Company trading post at Fort Ware, about 275 miles north of Prince George in the Rocky Mountain Trench. A veteran of the First World War, where he lost one leg below the knee, Ben also had a career as a rum runner during Prohibition before moving north to trap and, eventually, become a store keeper. I got to know Ben on our monthly mail and grocery trips to the fort. We couldn't just drop the mail and leave. We had to overnight while all the letters were answered and then fly out with the replies in the morning. It was during those overnight stays that I really got to know Ben.

He adopted both a benevolent and paternalistic attitude towards the First Nations people in the community, extending credit to everyone but doing everything in his power to keep them away from booze and the city. The former he accomplished by putting serious restrictions on the amount of yeast and raisins – prime home brew ingredients – anyone could buy. He didn't have quite as much control over the latter and more than once covered the cost of getting a Prince George reveller with empty pockets home to Fort Ware.

His store was the social centre of the community and a good place to keep warm in the winter. It was always busy in the mornings as the local women came and went, exchanging news and views, making their purchases and placing orders from the Eaton's catalogue. It was so busy

– people from Fort Grahame shopped there too – I always swore the till opened itself every time Ben passed a dollar bill close to it. The wooden tracks on the bottom of the cash drawer were smooth as glass. One of the most popular items for sale was chewing tobacco. Any pilot who forgot to include tobacco in the store's freight shipment was better off not landing as everyone, it seemed, from the age of 10 and up, had the habit.

The airline was not the only way to get freight into Fort Ware. It also came by boat and Art Van Somer was often at the helm. He captained an open riverboat 40 feet long and eight feet across that could carry four to five tons of freight. This was a back-breaking job as the boat had to be loaded by hand. There were rapids above Fort Grahame, just upriver from Finlay Forks, that were not passable in Art's fully-loaded boat. He would have to unload half the freight onto the shore, power up through the rapids, unload the remainder of his cargo, and then go back for what he'd left behind. He'd then have to navigate the rapids yet again, get the rest of his load and only then could he continue his journey upriver to Fort Ware.

*Bill and Toni on the frozen Finlay in March at Fort Ware.*

Ben openly welcomed almost all visitors to the village but there were some folk that made him a bit uneasy. Given his background in smuggling booze, he was leery of surprise visits by the RCMP. Any pilot who flew in without first announcing himself by radio would hear about it as soon as Ben emerged from hiding. And he was slow to warm to men of the cloth, anyone in fact who was trying to sell the local First Nations people another way of life. As far as Ben was concerned, the people had a perfectly good culture and spiritual life already. He never refused the clergy his hospitality but he did manage an arrangement that benefited him. He fed them and then let them sleep right in the store, near the woodstove. If they wanted to stay warm, they would have to keep the fire going and Ben, for a change, could sleep through the night. The only time I ever heard of Ben actually giving up his bed was one time when Toni came with me to the community.

I can't imagine Ben had much time, either, for the people behind the forced relocation of the Fort Ware children to residential schools like the one at Lejac, east of Fraser Lake. I was the pilot on some of those September pick up flights and was left in no doubt as to how the parents felt about the loss of their kids for the better part of every year. Of particular concern to the parents was their inability to teach their kids winter survival skills.

The harshness of the winters in Fort Ware and the hardiness of the people never failed to get my attention. In the cold mornings, when the temperature was sometimes minus 40 C, I got up early to warm the aircraft engine with my blow pots. There would be smoke coming from a few chimneys but most families had to wait for the man of the house to get up. He would then walk across the frozen river with his chainsaw and fetch home the day's wood supply.

When a hunter shot a moose, he didn't haul the carcass home. Instead, the family moved to the moose and lived there in tents until the meat was gone. It made sense in a way. The locations were always different, usually guaranteeing a good wood supply. And it was easier to get live people to the animal than to haul half a ton of dead meat home.

When Ben passed away in 1964 the only people at his funeral service were his kids, the PWA pilots and our wives, and Art Van Somer who had taken over the store. We couldn't get a minister to fly in to Fort Ware for the ceremony so we held it in Prince George. And since the minister had never met Ben, the service was rather brief. Fort Ware, now known as Kwadacha, is a thriving place today. There is road access and the children can go right through school to Grade 12 without ever leaving home.

# Heavy Loads

The heaviest thing I ever moved with an airplane was a D7 CAT. Ron Wells, another pilot with Trans-Provincial, two engineers, and I did it using two Otters on wheel skis and several thick, wooden planks on the floor of each plane. The contract called for us to move the big dozer from Burrage Creek, about 200 miles north of Terrace, to Snippaker Creek, about 35 minutes flying time to the west. The short distance meant we could carry less fuel, giving us more weight capacity for the parts.

The man in charge of dismantling the CAT had an excellent crew. As they took the machine apart, they weighed every piece using a scale mounted on a crane. Armed with that information we could make up loads of about 2,000 pounds each. Then we had to get the plane into the air. The strip at Burrage Creek has a deep gorge at either end. That meant we didn't have to fight to stay above the trees on takeoff but an engine failure would have been disastrous. The Burrage strip was ploughed so we used the wheels for takeoff and then put the skis down for landing at Snippaker. The Snippaker strip, built alongside a creek, had a distinct bend in the middle. Some fancy footwork on the rudder pedals was required if you wanted to avoid going into the creek.

We used a widening in one part of the Snippaker runway to unload the dozer parts but there was room for only one plane at a time on the actual strip. We tried to arrange things so that the empty plane had taken off from Snippaker before the loaded plane landed but on one occasion

*Bill and an Otter at rest.*

Ron took a bit longer to unload than usual and I had to land. I waited until he had pulled out of the loading area and was taxiing down the runway away from me. When he reached the end of the runway he would turn around and power up for takeoff. I was headed for the off-loading spot but hadn't quite made it as Ron came roaring down the runway towards me. I guess he figured there would be room to pass, or else he just couldn't see properly, but as he accelerated to takeoff speed, and I taxied down the strip towards him, I realized our right wings were going to hit. And because you can't just stop a plane on skis once there's forward momentum, a collision seemed inevitable. What happened next was nothing short of a miracle. Just as the two wings were about the smack into one another, Ron's right ski hit a snowy hummock on the runway and his right wing rose over the top of my wing. He completed his takeoff, headed back to Burrage Creek for another load and left me shaking in wonder.

While that incident left the planes unscathed, we were not so lucky when we transported the bulldozer's blade. The mechanics had welded some iron bars down the backside of the blade to hold it upright in Ron's plane. While his unloading assistant was trying to wedge the blade out of the plane with a big pry bar, the stabilizer bars broke off. The blade fell over, knocking the pry bar out of the assistant's hands and nearly crushing his legs before coming to rest against the metal framing of the heater duct. The assistant was able to climb out from behind the blade but the pry bar had punched a hole in the side of the plane. While all this was happening, I landed and taxied in behind Ron. Fortunately the damage to the Otter wasn't structural. We used jacks and winches to get the blade out of the plane and Ron then flew back to Burrage and patched up the hole.

Thanks to excellent weather it only took us a week to move the D7. There were a few other anxious moments associated with moving the bulldozer's winch and engine. Each of these items weighed about 2,900 pounds and we needed every inch of the Burrage runway, and a lot of nerve, to get the planes into the air. The mechanics put the bulldozer together in the spring and one of its first jobs was to straighten out the Snippaker runway.

The D7 move was not without incident but there was a cooperative and careful approach to that job. This was not the case when we were hired to move a D6 from the airstrip at Mackenzie to Black Lake, a site two hours away. That machine, once we got it moved, was used to build the Sturdee airstrip. I had a miserable load foreman for the job who was always pushing me to overload the aircraft. On one trip he tried to load over 5,000 pounds into the Otter. Had I not been keeping track, there's little doubt I would have crashed at the end of the runway.

During my time flying the Wenner-Gren mineral survey we sometimes stayed at Sawmill Lake, just north of the village of Telegraph Creek. The lake was suitable for small loads but heavy afternoon winds and cross currents made it too dangerous when working with bigger loads. So, when we were hired to move a large number of full fuel barrels from Telegraph Creek to Trapper Lake, about 60 miles to the west, I knew I'd have to fly off the Stikine River. I have landed on and taken off from big rivers – the Mackenzie, the Skeena, the Fraser – but none was as tricky as the Stikine, especially at the dock we used, just below the village.

It was a good dock but the river at that point is fast and narrow. On my first trip out with the Otter I was pointed upriver and knew I'd have to get turned around for takeoff into the wind. I got released from the dock and almost immediately realized I couldn't turn fast enough to get around before hitting the rocks on the far shore. Applying more power just hastened my trip to the rocks. That left me with only one option; I shut down the engine and let the wind turn the plane. It worked that time but I needed a better plan.

On subsequent trips I let the engine warm up at the dock, then untied the front rope and let the current swing the aircraft about 45 degrees before getting my helper to untie the back rope. I told him to keep an axe handy in case he had trouble with the rope and to cut it quick. The current at that point of the river could easily have broken the back off the float if the rope was still attached to it and the dock. This method worked well, especially on afternoons when there was a brisk, upriver wind. With the water flowing downstream at about 10 miles an hour and a 20-mile-an-hour wind at my nose, the plane would lift off the river in seconds. I would then turn and head upriver, flying close to the walls of the Stikine Canyon above the village, catching the updrafts created by the wind.

Landings on the river were a bit trickier. Every one of them had to be made flying upstream with the wind at my tail. If I landed downstream and into the wind, I would not have been able to get the plane turned around to get back to the dock. As some landings were made in a 25-mile-an-hour downwind approach, great care had to be taken to prevent the plane swinging back into the wind. If I allowed this to happen, the floats would be sideways to the current, pushing them downriver. The top of the plane would be sideways to the wind, which was pushing in the opposite direction. If the plane started to list, and the wind got under the wing, then the plane would capsize and the pilot would be swimming to shore. It was not a scenario I wanted to experience.

Trapper Lake, where we delivered the fuel drums, had a few peculiarities of its own. The wind was always from the west and caused a terrifically strong down draft right in the middle of the lake. I dealt with this by taking off into the wind and then circling to the left at about 10 feet off the surface and well before getting to the middle of the lake. I would then head down wind towards a steep cliff that rose from the northeast end of the lake. As I approached the cliff, an updraft would carry me to 8,000 feet in a turn and a half and I could be back to Telegraph in no time. I loved playing with the mountain winds but avoided it when carrying passengers. It was just too scary for them.

Before I leave the Stikine country I should mention this is grizzly bear country. I once landed on the river to pick up some hunters. They hadn't arrived so I beached the plane and was securing it to a tree when I noticed huge grizzly tracks just feet away from me. They were over a foot wide and one of them was still filling with water. The bear was very big and very close. I stayed close to the aircraft until my passengers arrived.

Another hauling job that tested my flying skills was moving 700 fuel barrels over two winters to the top of a 6,000-foot mountain north of Thutade Lake. Destined for a number of mining camps in the area, the barrels contained aviation gas, stove oil, diesel for the bulldozers and engine oil. Snow conditions were such we could sometimes offload the barrels and be on our way in half an hour. Other times the snow was so deep we had to tramp a solid-surfaced pad on which to unload the drums and then snowshoe a track to get the Otter airborne. Of course the weather had to be all but perfect for these trips. A nice sunny day would provide good visibility and create a shadow effect for approaches and landings. Whiteout conditions, however, meant you could over fly and go sliding down the backside of the mountain with a full load.

Another load I'll never forget was a small Bell bubble helicopter. It had crashed near a lake southwest of the Kenney Dam on the Nechako River and been dismantled by an insurance company engineer. It was my job to haul it out of the bush in pieces to a place where it could be repaired and put back into service. Easier said than done. We loaded the glass bubble, engine, blades, fuel tanks and other bits and pieces into the Otter and then tied the chopper's tube frame under a wing strut and on top of one of the floats. The load was well under the plane's weight limits and we had no trouble taking off into a stiff breeze.

That's when the trouble started. The plane kept veering to the left and I was having a lot of trouble climbing to a safe height above the trees. I circled the lake twice, trying to gain altitude, without success. The helicopter's fuselage, tied to the outside of the Otter, was creating a drag such as I'd never experienced before. I couldn't climb and I could not get my ground speed above 80 miles an hour.

I had a couple of choices. Either abort the flight or limp my way to the nearest road, which was at the Kenney Dam. I opted for the dam. It should have been a 15 minute flight but it took me a half hour. The grade was downhill so I was able to maintain my altitude and stay well above the trees at the same time. But it wasn't until the Ootsa Reservoir was in sight that I breathed easy. I was used to hauling boats and canoes on the Otter but this was a novel and distinctly unpleasant experience. No wonder those Bubble Bells were so slow.

Another example of an outside load causing considerable grief occurred one September. Pilot Scot Cameron and I were returning to Telkwa from Kitchener Lake with two Otters full of hunters, eight in all, and their game meat. We hit a storm as we approached Bear Lake and I followed a valley south to Babine Lake, touching down in the narrows near Smithers Landing. The valley leading into the Smithers area looked impassable. Scot tried to carry on to Granisle but weather turned him back. Both of us docked at Tukii Lodge and prepared to spend the night with owner Charlie Chaplin.

We had a great meal, and then played cards until about 10 p.m. At that point one of the hunters went to the outhouse and returned to report there were six inches of wet, sticky snow on the ground. My heart skipped a beat; both Scot and I jumped for the door at the same time and rushed outside. Both Otters had sunk to their tail fins under the weight of the snow. I grabbed a push broom, climbed up on the wing and started to remove the wet snow. After finishing one Otter I did the other. Meanwhile Scot pumped the water out of the submerged floats and by the time we finished, both planes were again resting at the proper angle in the water.

However, as I tried to climb down off the top of the aircraft, I slipped and tumbled right into the freezing lake, smashing one foot on a float as

*Dropping fuel barrels north of Thutade Lake at 6,000 feet.*

I fell. Helping hands got me onto the dock and I limped up to one of the cabins to change and warm up. By bedtime my right foot was bruised from the top of the arch to the bottom. The next morning I could not walk. One of the hunters lent me a snow boot to wear as I couldn't get my own shoes on the swollen foot. Around dusk a snow plough got through to the lodge and the hunters took a bus back to town. I didn't get back until the next day. While it wasn't broken, my foot was black and forced me to take a few days off work. Better, I guess, than having to lift two Otters off the bottom of the lake.

I carried another heavy load when I tried to get my Instrument Flight Rules, or IFR, licence in 1965. This was the licence a pilot needed if he was going to fly any of Pacific Western's scheduled passenger flights.

The training was conducted in Edmonton and was going quite well except for one thing. I was having a hard time connecting with any of the other guys – PWA captains and crew members with IFR status – who were part of the training and testing exercise. I'd always had great working and social relationships with other pilots so this bothered me, especially since one of those captains would be conducting my test. It was a bit of a mystery but I couldn't figure out what to do so I just carried on with my training.

We were using a war-surplus, twin-engine Anson with a heavy load of radios mounted in the nose of the aircraft. Radios in those days were big and heavy. This meant we carried some ballast in the rear of the Anson for balance. With two engines the power to weight ratio was fine but if an engine failed, we could be in trouble.

On the day of my test there were three of us on board – myself, a Department of Transport inspector and one of the PWA IFR captains – plus full fuel tanks. So now I had even more weight than during the training sessions. The first thing the captain asked me to do was fly on instruments and do 60-degree banks at a certain airspeed and hold my altitude. Basically this is a fighter pilot manoeuvre, had never even been discussed during training and is definitely not part of the repertoire for a pilot flying commercial passenger flights. But I tried it and did poorly.

The second test was to find my way back to the Edmonton airport and make an instrument approach to a specified runway. I did well on this, finding all the right beacons and was lining up for a landing when the DOT inspector failed an engine on me. With only one engine, and an overloaded aircraft, I had trouble maintaining minimum, basic altitude. "We're dead," said the PWA captain. "You've failed the test."

I was told later I'd made two basic mistakes. The first was ever taking off when I knew the plane was too heavy to fly safely on only one engine.

The second was trying the 60-degree banks. I should have refused, stating that I would never put my passengers at risk with such a manoeuvre unless it was absolutely necessary to avoid a mid-air collision.

It wasn't until later that I found out I'd been set up. The reason I'd had so much trouble connecting with the other PWA pilots was because I had too much seniority. In all of Pacific Western Airlines there were only 17 pilots who had more seniority with the company than I had. This meant that as soon as I obtained my IFR licence, I could displace or bump captains who were responsible for my testing. This was not a good situation and went a long way towards helping me understand what happened that day. I never tried for my IFR ticket again.

# Aircraft, Aircraft and More Aircraft

Listed below are all the aircraft I have flown and recorded in my logbook:

### *Cessna 140*

CF-EKR, CF-GII, CF-GDU

The 140 was the plane I used to get my private licence. It is a tail-wheel machine with a high wing. The seating is side by side with very little elbow room. The aircraft is all aluminum, has an 85 horsepower engine, cruises at about 100 miles per hour and has a range of 350 to 400 miles. I did a bit of ski work in Vernon with this aircraft but not enough to become a good ski pilot.

### *Cessna 180 and 185*

CF-HIW, CF-HLT, CF-HSP, CF-HYP, CF-JCQ, CF-UIG, CF-HYE, CF-PVH, CF-SZV, CF-OXE, CF-YYM

These aircraft were similar in size, but the 185 had a bigger engine. This made it capable of carrying a heavier payload. I flew the Cessnas for many years but if I had a choice between a 180 or a 185 and an Otter, I'd choose the Otter every time.

### *Cornell*

CF-FDL, CF-FDO

The Cornell was the first plane I owned. This machine was used as an air force trainer during the Second World War and later converted to

*Several Cornell PT26As just after the end of World War Two.* (Photo Courtesy of the Canadian Museum of Flight, Langley, BC)

civilian use. The Cornell is a low wing aircraft with a tail wheel. The gear did not retract as in some trainers of this type. It was powered by a 225 horse Ranger engine. Fuel consumption was quite high so I took friends who would help with the gas whenever I flew. Terry, one of the friends who flew with me, liked the plane so much she cleaned it on a regular basis.

### *Beech 17*

CF–GKW

This was a bi-plane with a Pratt and Whitney R985 engine. It would fly nearly 200 miles an hour on wheels and cruised at about 145 miles an hour on floats. It was a metal tube covered with fabric and had a very sleek and fast look to it. I really enjoyed flying the Beech. It flew like a fighter and I would dearly like to have flown one on wheels. Jack Moul, another of the PWA pilots in Port Alberni, also loved to fly this aircraft. He said it was the closest thing to the Spitfires he had flown during the war. This machine was lighter than other R 985 powered aircraft and the acceleration was exhilarating.

### *Seabee*

CF–FLV

This high winged aircraft is a flying boat with retractable landing gear for water landings and wheels for airport runways. I flew this plane for a few months out of Powell River. It had a 250 horsepower, pusher engine and the prop was reversing, enabling a pilot to back away from a dock. This was handy around pilings and congested harbours. I used this machine for my first true commercial flying. It handled well but glided like a brick if you lost the engine.

### *Fairchild 71*

CF–BXI

The Fairchild was a high wing machine with a 450 horsepower Pratt and Whitney engine. It swung a nine-foot metal prop that produced good takeoff and cruise capabilities. It was rated for about 1,500 pounds of cargo but often carried more.

The Fairchild worked mostly on floats but it was a good ski machine as well. It was a long machine with a narrow body and seating in the cockpit for the pilot only. This meant you had to have a brave check out pilot who would stand just back of the trainee pilot and hope he did everything right on his first check ride.

*A Travelair.*

### *Travelair*

CF–AEJ

The Travelair had much the same build as the Fairchild but had a wider cabin and was not as long. It was powered by a Pratt and Whitney

R985 engine and carried the same prop as the Fairchild. Both aircraft were tube construction with a fabric covering. The wings were wood and covered with fabric. I flew this aircraft from Burns Lake to West Tahtsa a lot when the construction of the Kemano project was at its peak. The Travelair was considered by Charles Lindberg when he was looking for a plane for his famous New York to Paris flight over the Atlantic. The one I flew was one of only 14 Travelairs and PWA eventually sold it to a charter outfit in Alaska.

*A Norseman flying in good weather on the coast.*

### Norseman

Mark 4—CF–CRS CF–DFU

Mark 5—CF–OBG CF–OBR CF–GUM CF– BHZ CF–BHU

Mark 6—CF–FAA CF–GSK CF–GOB

This tube-construction aircraft with fabric covering was built in Montreal and intended for work in the Canadian bush. There were three models made: the Mark IV, V, and VI. The latter was made for the air force during the war, was a much heavier aircraft and did not perform as well as the earlier Mark IV and V versions

The Norseman had a 600 horsepower R1430 engine and would carry 10 people or a ton of freight. Most of my flying on the west coast was done with a Norseman on floats but I did log a few hours flying one on skis to the Williston Reservoir area. The Norseman did not have a good glide ratio. A pilot needed lots of altitude in the event of an engine failure – about 800 feet to do a 180-degree turn before landing.

Every Norseman had its own idiosyncrasies. Some were nose heavy and others tail heavy. Some you could land on a small lake and get out again easily. With others, you never knew if you would clear the trees on takeoff.

### *DHC–2 Beaver*

CF–ICL, CF–FHB, CF–GYM, CF–GQC, CF–FHN, CF–ICK, CF–EYS, CF–GCY, CF–GQN, CF–JXQ, CF–JHE, CF–GYM, CF–JOS, CF–OBU, CF–DSU, CF–OCH

This was the first good bush plane made in Canada by de Havilland. It was powered by a 450 horsepower R985 Pratt & Whitney engine. As this was the engine used to power several twin-engine aircraft during World War Two, there were hundreds on hand for use by de Havilland. The Beaver was the first true short takeoff and landing (STOL) aircraft. It had a great flap system that enabled it to land at lower landing speed and also get off the water quickly, making it possible to venture into smaller lakes where other, older aircraft would never dare go. It was built of aluminum and either painted or just polished. Sometimes a few stripes were added to enhance the appearance.

CF–FHB was the first Beaver built and all the testing was done on this one machine. The aircraft was put into civilian use in 1948 when Russ Baker bought it from de Havilland. The Beaver I flew most often was CF–ICL. This aircraft was originally owned by Jim Spilsbury and came over to Russ Baker when he bought Spilsbury's Queen Charlotte Airlines. It was CF–ICL I used for two and a half years while flying the Wenner-Gren survey.

### *DHC-3 Otter*

CF–XUY, CF–RNO, CF–KLC, CF–GCV

These aircraft had a geared 600 horsepower R1430 engine swinging an 11-foot diameter, three-bladed prop. The cabin was much too big for the aircraft and frequently resulted in overloads as people tried to fill all that extra space. The flap system on this machine made it super STOL. It could actually outperform the smaller Beaver on small lakes and fields.

The first one I flew was CF–GCV which was only the second Otter built by de Havilland. The Otter was my favourite aircraft to fly, even though it required a lot of work to load it properly. I logged more time in the Otter than any other machine, using it on wheels, floats and skis and eventually discovered its amazing capabilities. But you have to know how to load it if you are to get the best performance from this machine. Some pilots never learned and staggered through the air.

### *Junkers*

CF–AQW, CF–ATF, CF–AQB

This was a German aircraft with corrugated, aluminum skin. It would carry a ton of freight and had a cruise range of about 600 miles. Some of them came from the factory in Germany with a water-cooled, in-line engine which was replaced with a Pratt and Whitney R1430 in Canada.

### *Anson*

CF–PAC

Two Pratt and Whitney R985 engines powered this aircraft. The body and wings were plywood and covered with fabric and dope. These were purchased from war assets, converted to civilian use and many of them were used for the DEW Line contract.

I did my instrument flight training in an Anson at the PWA base in Edmonton. I never did a commercial flight in one of these aircraft but remember being a passenger in one that was delivering flowers from Vernon to Vancouver one year when the Fraser Valley was flooded from side to side.

### *Widgeon*

CF–SPA, CF–BVN

This aircraft was the smaller flying boat made by the Grumman Aircraft Company, the bigger version being the Goose. The Widgeon was powered by two 190 horsepower Lycoming engines and had room for two flight crew and five passengers. The metal construction made for a very sturdy but heavy machine. Wheel landings were very easy and this was a nice aircraft to fly but tricky on the water as it had a strong tendency to porpoise.

*Bill in the pilot's seat of a Grumman Widgeon.*

### *Apache*

CF-KXL

This is a twin engine aircraft with a low wing made of metal. It has two 150 horsepower Lycoming engines and the landing gear is of the nose wheel type and retracts for cruising. I flew it a few times out of Prince George and enjoyed its flying qualities.

### *Piper Super Cub*

CF-JUE

This was a high-wing, fabric-covered machine with tandem seating for two. We used it mostly for prospectors looking for likely mineral deposits. It was also a good aircraft for game counting as it could be used low and slow and the visibility was good on both sides of the aircraft for pilot and passenger.

### *Karatoo*

C-GBLI

This is an aircraft that I built from a set of plans over seven winters. It is a high wing machine with side-by-side seating with a set of floats made of carbon and Kevlar fibres. These floats are of my own design, and have given good performance. The engine is a Subaru with about 90 horsepower. I put a ground adjustable prop on it made of carbon fibres. It is a fun aircraft but has no payload capacity; a big lunch bag makes a full load when you're carrying full fuel tanks and a passenger. I later carved my own 84-inch diameter prop from laminated birch. It provided a very good take-off but the cruise remained the same as with the carbon prop.

*Bill at the controls of his homebuilt Karatoo on Tyhee Lake.*
(Photo courtesy of Don Burton)

I have flown other aircraft that never made it into my log book. These were usually just familiarization flights and involved a Tiger Moth, a bi-plane used for training World War Two pilots, and an Aeronca owned by a friend in Vernon. I also did a check flight in a Grumman Goose and crewed on a Grumman Mallard from Vancouver to Kitimat.

Compared with today's bush flying, my 30-plus years was seat-of-the-pants stuff. We had no global positioning system (GPS) to tell us how far and in which direction it was to our next landing site. We used a map, a ruler and did the arithmetic in our heads. In the Arctic, where compasses were of no value, the sun and a good watch were used to set the directional gyroscope. On dull days, if we were lucky and could tune into a radio transmitter on the loop antenna, we could set the gyro that way.

With GPS, computers and satellite maps, getting a reliable weather forecast quickly is much easier today. My generation of bush pilots kept an eye on the evening sky as an indicator of the next day's weather. We listened for the squawking and flying of loons and, on the coast, watched for an inland migration of seagulls as signs of impending bad weather.

Today's turbine engines are lighter, more reliable and more powerful than the piston engines of old. The extra power triples the rate of climb, thus enabling the pilot to get out of harm's way much more quickly, something I could have made good use of when flying the mineral survey. I still can't believe we were able to complete the mineral survey, and without incident, using the equipment we had.

But do I regret any of it? No. It was true bush flying where caution, intuition, experience, resourcefulness, endurance and a keen eye kept you productive and alive, most of the time, and I wouldn't have traded it for anything. And, I'm pretty sure, neither would any of the bush pilots who flew with me. We are a special breed.

# Acknowledgements

This book would never have found its way into your hands had it not been for the patience and prolific memory of my wife Toni. Not only did she keep our home and raise our kids during my frequent and sometimes prolonged absences, she has been the keeper of many of the stories that were never recorded in my flight logs. That they have been shared here is down to her. I also wish to thank those responsible for the Elder College program at Northwest Community College in Smithers and Walter Hromatka for their guidance in book preparation. Thanks also to Mark Edwards, for unravelling some of the mysteries of the computer, to Don Parminter for the cover map, Lynn Shervill and Sheila Peters for their work in editing and design, and to Bruce Apps, Gordon Williams and George Flieger for some of the photos used in this book. And finally, by way of thanks to my children, I give them the last word. Here's what they had to say about growing up as children of a bush pilot.

**Randy**

I was born in Vancouver but never actually lived in a big city until I went to university. Instead I lived in some of the exotic locales to which Dad was posted for work – like Fort St. James where, as an infant, I used to sleep in a dresser drawer in a cabin on the government dock.

When I was a youngster, Dad frequently took me along when he flew fishermen to remote lakes in the northern half of the province. In most cases those lakes, and the streams flowing into them, had been fished only rarely. This meant I caught a trout on every second or third cast. Easy fishing – no skill or patience required. But Dad made me clean them which definitely served to limit the number I hooked.

As I got older I spent a lot of time hanging around float plane docks. Sometimes I helped unload the planes Dad flew. I remember one time we were unloading full fuel barrels from an Otter and using a ramp to roll them onto the shore. Dad misjudged the line on one barrel and it flipped, prematurely, off the ramp and into the water right beside me, soaking me from head to toe. When I looked up he was standing in the plane's doorway, laughing at my impromptu shower.

By the time I was a teenager, and still hanging around the docks, I was receiving lots of job offers to work in various bush camps. In 1969 a guide-outfitter offered me $300 for the summer to work as a camp hand and novice wrangler. I was all set to sign on when a mining exploration company offered me $300 a month to carry a backpack for one of the university consultants. That job turned into work for seven consecutive summers with different mining companies across northern BC and into the Yukon.

So, in a way, it's thanks to Dad I got those jobs. But he benefited too. I made enough to pay my own way through university.

**Gary**

Growing up as the son of a bush pilot was a gift. I spent my early life at the boundary between wilderness and civilization, moving between the small urban centres we called home and the coastal and northern wilds where my father worked. At 18 I moved to Vancouver and the University of British Columbia where I had to shift to a fully urban and academic lifestyle. This somewhat transient and paradoxical existence prepared me well for a career that has taken me around the world, exposed to a variety of societies and cultures.

I was born in Port Alberni but my first recollection of life is from Prince George where Dad was flying Otters and Beavers for Pacific Western Airlines. Summers were his busiest times so we saw the least of him during those months. Winters were less hectic in terms of flying but he filled the time with a variety of do-it-yourself projects, often enlisting the aid of his children. I recall many hours spent in the construction of boats and mini-bikes and the repair of various household appliances. Winter freeze-ups (November through December) and spring thaws (April through May) were the down times for bush pilots. Consequently, these were the times when we took family holidays.

Some of my favourite times were trips into remote fishing and mining camps and swimming off the floats attached to a variety of bush planes. I actually got to spend a whole week with Dad in the summer of 1967. It was very hot and there was a huge forest fire near Chetwynd north of Prince George. I flew with him every day as we scooped up water from various lakes and dumped it on the burning trees. It was the experience of a lifetime. And staying in the forward fire fighting camps was a dream-come-true. These camps were generously stocked with what some might refer to as junk food. For me, it was like living in paradise.

In 1968 we moved to Telkwa, a small town about 400 kilometres northwest of Prince George and the place I still think of as home. We lived about two kilometres from the Trans-Provincial Airlines base on Tyhee Lake. If Dad was going to make it home for supper he would buzz the house before landing and we'd know to wait for him. From Telkwa Dad flew into some of the most beautiful places on the planet. I have visited more than 70 countries around the world in my career as a cardiovascular scientist but the Spatsizi, Babine Lake and the Nass Valley still rank near the top of my list of favourites. It was thanks to Dad that I ever got to see them in the first place. I thank him too for the summer jobs in fishing camps, learning the skills of wilderness survival and all that time wielding an axe. I wouldn't trade the experience of growing up the son of a bush pilot for anything.

**Lynn**

As I grew up it was always with a sense that my dad had a very special job. I often heard adventure stories when other pilots came over and sometimes had the thrill of flying with him on some of his short hauls.

And, like my brothers, I thank Dad for those summer jobs. Mine, with the BC Forest Service, kept me solvent through university.

Raised with discipline and a strong work ethic, I know that my dad did not expect anything of my brothers or myself that he wasn't willing to deliver himself. He didn't fool us though; we know he had a real soft spot as proven by the Nipper story. Of all Dad's stories, that one continues to be my favourite.

Like he did with all his passengers, Dad delivered his three children safely to their adult destinations. I'm very proud of you, Dad.